SCHOLASTIC

10 MUST-HAVE Text Sets

Thought-Provoking Packs to Foster Critical Thinking & Collaborative Discussion

Carol Pugliano-Martin

New York • Toronto • London • Auckland • Sydney
Mexico City • New Delhi • Hong Kong • Buenos Aires

Dedication

To my amazing students and colleagues at New Lebanon School for your contributions to this book. Read it! Some of you are quoted!

And to my wonderful family—Scott, Baxter, Hayden, and Drake. Working on this book was like having another child, and you all welcomed him/her with open arms!

Photos ©: cover background: rzarek/Shutterstock, Inc.; cover main: Tetra Images/Shutterstock, Inc.; 14: tomwang/Can Stock Photo, Inc.; 15: eldadcarin/Thinkstock; 30: jabejon/iStockphoto; 31: Courtesy Taylor Elementary School; 32: huePhotography/iStockphoto; 36: Hector Retamal/Getty Images; 37: TOLES © 2005 The Washington Post. Reprinted with permission of Universal Uclick. All rights reserved.; 38: clayc3466/iStockphoto; 39: juuce/iStockphoto; 43: Alejandro Rivera/iStockphoto; 48: Mooneydriver/iStockphoto; 49: Rich Legg/iStockphoto; 50: NASA; 52: Hulton Archive/Getty Images; 53: NASA/Getty Images; 58: Danita Delimont/Getty Images; 61: Universal History Archive/Getty Images; 62: Burstein CollecCon/Corbis Images; 63: AS400 DB/Corbis Images; 66: traveler1116/iStockphoto; 68: Hulton Archive/Getty Images; 77: Don Troiani/Corbis Images; 79: Bloomberg/Getty Images; 81: Hulton Archive/Getty Images; 82: Stock Montage/Getty Images; 84: benoitb/iStockphoto; 85: MPI/Getty Images; 89 top and throughout: GeorgiosArt/iStockphoto; 89 bottom and throughout: GeorgiosArt/iStockphoto; 92: leezsnow/iStockphoto.

Editor: Sarah Glasscock
Cover design by Michelle H. Kim
Interior design by Holly Grundon
Copy editor: Eileen Judge

ISBN: 978-0-545-75190-2
Copyright © 2016 by Carol Pugliano-Martin
All rights reserved.
Printed in the U.S.A.
First printing, June 2016.

1 2 3 4 5 6 7 8 9 10   40   22 21 20 19 18 17 16

Contents

Theme: Historical Events

Introduction

I am like you—"in the trenches," as they say. I am currently in my tenth year of teaching. For all of these years, and in the years preceding those when I worked in educational publishing, I have seen many educational buzzwords and practices come and go. Every year, it seems there is the next big thing. Sometimes it's hard for teachers (as well as administrators, parents, and students) to keep up.

As of this writing, 46 states have adopted the Common Core State Standards. Among the changes called for are an expanded role of nonfiction texts and the practice of close reading with the use of text evidence to answer higher-level questions. While a few states have withdrawn from (or are considering dropping) the Common Core, many are replacing them with similar standards.

Teachers all around the country are scrambling to find materials that can be used to help students meet and even exceed these challenging standards. I am one of those teachers. Like you, I spend a lot of time searching for the perfect short text that will lend itself to one or more of the standards.

10 Must-Have Text Sets came out of a unit of study on multiple perspectives I did with a small group of fifth graders. One of my biggest challenges was finding age-appropriate nonfiction texts that could be used to direct students to focus on different perspectives, points of view, and author's purpose. Each topic in this book is covered from two or more perspectives, allowing for lively conversations and debates to take place in your classroom.

This book is geared toward Grades 3–6, but a review of the standards shows that the strands I am focusing on extend into later middle school as well. The text sets in this book are correlated to the Common Core State Standards on page 7.

CCSS CORRELATIONS

Grade 3

RI.3.1 Ask and answer questions to demonstrate understanding of a text, referring explicitly to the text as a basis for the answers.

RI.3.6 Distinguish their own point of view from that of the author of a text.

RI.3.9 Compare and contrast the most important points and key details presented in two texts on the same topic.

Grade 4

RI.4.1 Refer to details and examples in a text when explaining what the text says explicitly and when drawing inferences from the text.

RI.4.6 Compare and contrast a first-hand and second-hand account of the same event or topic, describe the differences in focus and the information provided.

RI.4.8 Explain how an author uses reasons and evidence to support particular points in a text.

Grade 5

RI.5.1 Quote accurately from a text when explaining what the text says explicitly and when drawing inferences from the text.

RI.5.3 Explain the relationships or interactions between two or more individuals, events, ideas, or concepts in historical, scientific, or technical text based on specific information in the text.

RI.5.6 Analyze multiple accounts of the same event or topic, noting important similarities and differences in the point of view they represent.

RI.5.9 Integrate information from several texts on the same topic in order to write or speak about the subject knowledgeably.

Grade 6

RI.6.1 Cite textual evidence to support analysis of what the text says explicitly as well as inferences drawn from the text.

RI.6.2 Determine a central idea of a text and how it is conveyed through particular details; provide a summary of the text distinct from personal opinions or judgments.

RI.6.3 Analyze in detail how a key individual, event, or idea is introduced, illustrated, and elaborated in a text (e.g., through examples or anecdotes).

RI.6.6 Determine an author's point of view or purpose in a text and explain how it is conveyed in the text.

RI.6.7 Integrate information presented in different media or formats (e.g., visually, quantitatively) as well as in words to develop a coherent understanding of a topic or issue.

RI.6.8 Trace and evaluate the argument and specific claims in a text, distinguishing claims that are supported by reasons and evidence from claims that are not.

RI.6.9 Compare and contrast one author's presentation of events with that of another (e.g., a memoir written by and a biography on the same person).

About Text Sets

A text set is a group of texts organized around a common topic. An anchor text introduces the topic, and the other texts in the set relate to the topic in some way. Through close readings of all the texts in the set, students develop a deeper understanding of the topic and the vocabulary associated with it. A text set may contain a variety of genres; for example, Text Set 10 on the ratification of the United States Constitution consists of a magazine article, an original play, a diagram describing the three branches of government, and the Bill of Rights. Text sets encourage students to analyze, compare, and synthesize the information about the topic, and these essential skills will help them meet the expectations of the CCSS or your states' rigorous standards.

How to Use This Book

The text sets in this book feature written work in a variety of genres as well as links to video clips,* artwork, and editorial cartoons for students to analyze. These text sets lend themselves to a range of instructional units, including nonfiction and opinion writing. You can also incorporate text sets into units with related content. For example, if you are doing a science unit on space, Text Set 6: Why Explore Space? will add a trans-disciplinary element to your lessons. While the texts here are meant to be used as sets, you can also pull out a specific article for a lesson on summarizing or finding the main idea and details of a text. The video links can also be used to help students hone their listening skills and practice taking notes.

This book is divided into thematic sections. It begins with a section on issues that affect kids at school. This is followed by text sets that focus on current events. The final section highlights historic events and periods in American history. Every text in a set has "Think About It" questions to spark critical thinking and discussion. These questions can be answered by students individually, in small groups, or as a whole class. And depending on your instructional goals, students can respond in writing or through discussion. A graphic organizer, which students can use to organize their writing and discussion, closes each text set.

---

*NOTE: Always check the links prior to letting students access them online as the content of websites might change over time.

Notes About Individual Text Sets

The level of primary sources may seem too high for some students, but I felt it was important to present the person's actual words. The accompanying introductions and/or explanations to the primary sources will help students navigate these challenging texts. As with all the texts, you may want to preview them for key vocabulary that students may be unfamiliar with or may find challenging.

Text Set 1: Getting Paid for Good Grades You can have students read the play "Should Kids Get Paid for Good Grades?" (page 17) on their own or ask each student in a group to take a part.

Text Set 4: Animals in Captivity At the National Zoo in Washington, D.C., several animals died in 2015, including a pygmy hippopotamus, a cheetah, two red pandas, and a bobcat. There has been speculation that the animals might have died of neglect, which is reflected in the cartoon (page 37), depicting the veterinary staff asleep. Do not show students the explanation of the cartoon above. Show them only the cartoon and give them ample time to analyze it and try to figure out its message and stance.

Text Set 7: The "First" Thanksgiving Present the two written accounts of the first Thanksgiving, then the paintings, along with the Think About It questions.

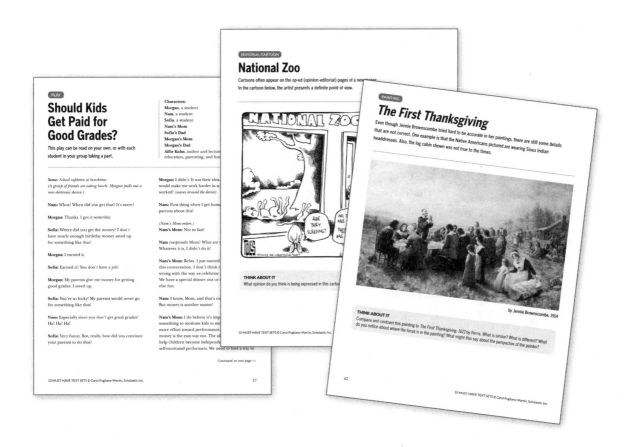

Activities to Use With the Text Sets

You can use the following activities to supplement your teaching of these text sets. I have used many of them with my students, and they have been very successful in opening up students' minds to look at issues critically.

One of the main concepts in working with text sets is to expose students to multiple perspectives on one issue. Young people (and adults!) often see issues as being black or white, as having a definite right or wrong. Students may need some supplemental practice in seeing things from different points of view. Activities 1–3 work well as an introduction to exploring multiple perspectives. The other activities are designed for use during a unit or as a culmination.

1. Mystery Guest: This is a fun way to begin a unit on multiple perspectives. Plan ahead to have another teacher or staff member enter your classroom while you are teaching. That person should come in, walk around the room—maybe lifting objects, looking around. He or she might whisper something in your ear. After about 30 seconds of moving around the room doing odd things, the person should simply walk out. Tell the class to freeze, and pass out index cards. Unfreeze students and ask them to write down what they just saw. Chances are, students' responses will be very different. Some may try to guess what the person was doing in the classroom. Some may describe exactly what they saw. When students have finished, gather the cards and share all of them to show how different people can look at the same event in different ways. Draw a circle in the middle of chart paper and write the event inside (e.g., Mrs. C. comes into the room). Then write the different comments around the center. Some of my students' comments were: "She's making the room more technological." (Mrs. C. was our media specialist.) "She's fixing a printer." "I'm so confused." "She looked suspicious."

2. The Whole Picture: Cut out pieces of close-up pictures of objects, such as vegetables, animals, flowers, or tools. Put a divider between partners and then give each one a piece of the same picture. Tell students not to look at each other's picture piece. Have students write down what they think their piece of the picture shows. Then have partners compare notes. Next, challenge them to figure out the whole image by putting their pieces together. Finally, give partners the image with their pieces cut out. The purpose of this activity is to show students that they have to consider every part of an issue to get the whole picture. I gave one group a close-up picture of a cat's face. One student got a piece of the cat's nose. She thought it was a squid. Her partner got a whisker. He thought it was someone's nose hair seen through a microscope!

3. Picture This: A good way to scaffold instruction on multiple perspectives is to start with picture books before moving on to complicated nonfiction. There are many wonderful picture books that lend themselves to viewing issues through multiple perspectives. Here are a few I have found useful:

- *Voices in the Park* by Anthony Browne
- *Hey, Little Ant* by Phillip and Hannah Hoose
- *Fish Is Fish* by Leo Lionni
- *The Little House* by Virginia Lee Burton
- *Seven Blind Mice* by Ed Young
- *The True Story of the Three Little Pigs* by Jon Scieszka
- *Mirror Mirror* by Marilyn Singer

4. Opposing Opinions: Sometimes it is difficult enough to defend our own point of view. Imagine having to defend an opposing view! Try this with your students: Have them choose an issue they feel strongly about. Encourage students to write an opinion piece about their perspective on the issue. Then challenge them to write an opposing opinion. I usually ask students to present both of their opinion pieces to an audience. The audience members then vote on which view they think a student actually holds. To close, each student presents a short, original skit that reveals his or her true opinion. Some of my students were so convincing, the audience was sure they felt the opposite of their true opinion.

5. What's Your Perspective? After learning about an issue, invite groups or individual students to take on different perspectives and be interviewed by the rest of the class. For example, my class read an article on having in-car cameras to monitor teenagers' driving. The class was divided into groups. One group read and annotated the article as though they were the teenagers affected by this topic. Another group took on a parent's perspective. Yet another group viewed the issue from the perspective of police officers. After the groups had time to read, annotate, and discuss, each one formulated interview questions to ask the other groups. Then each group was interviewed by the others.

6. Try to See It My Way: A good way for students to put themselves in another's shoes is for them to write a journal entry as that person. This works well when exploring characters in fiction, but is also beneficial when looking at a real event. I used this activity to explore the Taino Indians and Columbus encountering one another. We looked at the landing from the perspective of Columbus and his crew and also from the perspective of the Taino Indians. The students wrote journal entries as the Taino Indians, exploring how they may have felt about meeting the strangers. This activity can be done with any issue, historical or current. It is naturally more of a challenge when there are no written records of one side's perspective, such the Tainos or the Wampanoag Indians. (See Text Set 7: The "First" Thanksgiving.) Students usually come up with interesting, yet realistic, perspectives.

7. Mock Trial: Create a mock trial surrounding one of the issues in this book or another issue your students find interesting and relevant. You may have a judge, a defendant and lawyer, a plaintiff and prosecutor, a jury, and expert witnesses who give testimony. You can also add a court stenographer and a bailiff to make the trial even more realistic! Court reporters and members of the audience can also provide crucial views of the trial and the issues.

8. This Is How I See It: Before students begin analyzing nonfiction texts for perspective, point of view, and so on, read a selection of short stories and analyze them. Make a copy of the selections for each student. Have students read all the stories either in class or as homework. After reading the stories, break students into groups. Give each group a different story from the selection and have them work together to rewrite an abridged version of the story from a different character's perspective. For example, if the story is written from the perspective of a child, the group rewrites it from the parent's point of view. Most students will be familiar with the concept, as there are many "retold" stories published, such as the Wolf's take on the Three Little Pigs. Each group shares its version with the class. Since all students have read each story, they will better understand how the shifting perspective changes the story, or at least puts a different spin on it.

* * *

Thank you for doing what you do. I hope this book helps you cut out a lot of the legwork involved in finding material for your lessons so you can focus on what matters the most—your students!

GETTING PAID FOR GOOD GRADES

Several years ago, I taught a fourth-grade advanced language arts class in which my students had to choose a topic to research and write about. They chose the issue of paying students for getting good grades. The topic was very engaging for them, and it was interesting to see that, even though the idea itself appealed to them, they were able to view it from multiple sides rather than letting their personal views get the better of them. As a result, my students were able to write very well-informed and unbiased essays.

TEXTS

Should Students Be Paid for Good Grades?

Do you like getting rewarded for doing good things? Most kids do. Stickers, prizes—even money—can often motivate kids to do things, such as getting good grades. But some experts think that rewarding kids in this way is a bad idea.

Want a way to make some good money? Just get good grades! That's what some schools around the country are doing. Some think it is a brilliant tool for hard-to-motivate students. Others think it is bribery that will destroy any chance of fostering a love of learning. A recent study has found that paying kids for good grades gets results. It helps low-income students stay in school and get better grades.

This theory was tested in Louisiana, at two community colleges. The program required students to enroll in college, maintain at least a "C" average, and then they would earn $1000 a semester for up to two terms. Participants were 30 percent more likely to register for a second semester than students who were not offered the financial reward. But they didn't just sign up for another semester, they were also more likely to maintain a "C" average than students who did not participate. They also reported feeling better about themselves and their abilities to accomplish their goals for the future.

Some critics are concerned that cash rewards will encourage students to start taking easier classes to make sure they do well enough to earn the money. Kirabo Jackson, an assistant professor at Cornell University, is one of those critics. "By rewarding people for a GPA [Grade Point Average], you're actually giving them an impetus to take an easier route through college," he says.

Arnel Cosey, from New Orleans' Delgado Community College, says she understands why some people are concerned that cash incentives are nothing more than bribery. "But on the other hand," she says, "I'm not sure that I'm opposed to bribing. If that's what we need to do for these people to reach these goals, I wish I had more money to give." Besides, as Cosey adds, if all goes well, students will be getting cash incentives for their work soon after graduating—in the form of a paycheck. "Most of us wouldn't turn up at work every day if we weren't getting a check," she says. "What's wrong with starting the payment a little early?"

THINK ABOUT IT
Would you work harder in school if you received money for good grades? Explain why or why not.

Should I pay my kids for good grades?

BY CHRISTINA VERCELLETTO

Parents want to do the right thing. But often it's hard to know what the right thing is. One parent asked an expert. Here is her advice.

Q: Should I pay my kid for good grades?

A: "Rewards do work," says child development expert Michelle Anthony, Ph.D. "Dinner out, a movie, even money can change your child's thinking from 'I can't do this' to 'How can I make it happen?'" However, there are two important things to keep in mind. First, make sure the goals you set can be reached (saying you'll only pay for A's might be too tough). Second, change the rewards from time to time. If you use the same reward every time, your child may start asking for more of that same reward to keep working hard. –C.V.

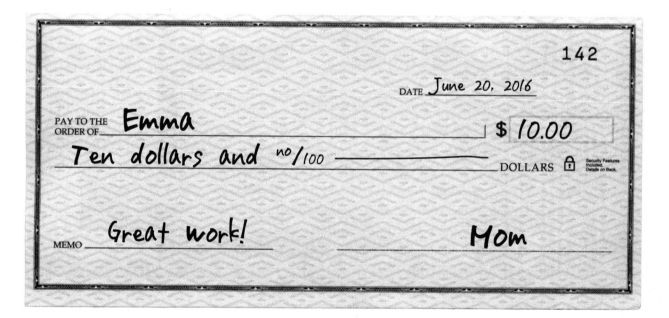

THINK ABOUT IT

Write a list of rewards you would like, besides money, to suggest to your parents.

Motivation: The Secret Behind Student Success

BY DANA TRUBY

Scholastic Instructor magazine talked to Daniel Pink, best-selling author and expert on business, work, and management, to get his ideas on the best way to motivate and reward kids.

Don't we all value rewards?

Pink: Science tells us that "if-then" rewards—if you do this, then you get that—do work for simple tasks. They worked in the 20th century when many people worked in factories.

Now we're preparing kids for the jobs of the future.

Pink: Certainly. Now our work tasks are more complex. Solving complex problems requires an inquiring mind and the willingness to experiment one's way to a fresh solution.

How do rewards work against motivation?

Pink: When you say, "If you get an A on this test, I'll give you $5," that's a colossal mistake. What that says is the only purpose of getting an A on a test is to get a reward. It puts the focus on getting the reward and not on the work itself.

What would you say to schools that claim to have found success by paying for grades?

Pink: In general, I opposed it, but I'm willing to reserve judgment for kids who have no real understanding of what learning is. If it takes a little bit of a bribe to get that kid to open up a book, then it's hard to argue that that's a bad idea. But, there's research being done in New York City and some other places about whether those sorts of methods are effective even for the most disadvantaged kids.

Can rewards ever be done well in school?

Pink: For the vast majority of kids, most rewards are a disaster. At the same time, if your students do well on a test and you say, "Hey, you really worked hard. You really learned a lot. You mastered algebra, and to celebrate, let's have a pizza party," that's not really the same thing because the party isn't based on the kids' performance. The danger, however, is if kids begin to say, "Every time I do well on a test I get a pizza party."

So I think that in general, rewards should be in the form of feedback and information and, sometimes, praise.

> **THINK ABOUT IT**
> Daniel Pink calls rewards a "disaster." What does he mean? Use your own words.

Should Kids Get Paid for Good Grades?

This play can be read on your own, or with each student in your group taking a part.

Characters:
Morgan, a student
Nam, a student
Sofia, a student
Nam's Mom
Sofia's Dad
Morgan's Mom
Morgan's Dad
Alfie Kohn, author and lecturer in areas of education, parenting, and human behavior

---

Scene: School cafeteria at lunchtime
(A group of friends are eating lunch. Morgan pulls out a new electronic device.)

Nam: Whoa! When did you get that? It's sweet!

Morgan: Thanks. I got it yesterday.

Sofia: Where did you get the money? I don't have nearly enough birthday money saved up for something like that!

Morgan: I earned it.

Sofia: Earned it? You don't have a job!

Morgan: My parents give me money for getting good grades. I saved up.

Sofia: You're so lucky! My parents would never go for something like that!

Nam: Especially since you don't get good grades! Ha! Ha! Ha!

Sofia: Very funny. But, really, how did you convince your parents to do that?

Morgan: I didn't. It was their idea. They thought it would make me work harder in school, and I guess it worked! *(waves around the device)*

Nam: First thing when I get home, I'm telling my parents about this!

(Nam's Mom enters.)
Nam's Mom: Not so fast!

Nam *(surprised)*: Mom? What are you doing here? Whatever it is, I didn't do it!

Nam's Mom: Relax. I just wanted to comment on this conversation. I don't think there is anything wrong with the way *we* celebrate good grades. We have a special dinner out or do something else fun.

Nam: I know, Mom, and that's cool and all. But money is another matter!

Nam's Mom: I do believe it's important to find something to motivate kids to study harder and put more effort toward performance. But I feel that money is the easy way out. The ultimate goal is to help children become independent learners and self-motivated performers. We need to find a way to

Continued on next page >>

enhance self-pride rather than reward them from outside. I believe it's good to celebrate outcomes, but keep it appropriate with a favorite meal or family outing. Of course, that's just my two cents. No pun intended!

Sofia: Ha! Ha! Ha! I guess she told you!

(Sofia's Dad appears.)
Sofia's Dad: Well, hello!

Sofia *(surprised)*: Dad? This is weird!

Sofia's Dad: I'm not sure how I feel about this whole paying-for-good-grades thing.

Sofia: But how are you . . . ? How did you . . . ?

Sofia's Dad: I think this is a bad bargain in many ways. You students must value education. Giving you bribes is corrupting that value.

Morgan: With all due respect, sir, it's not really a bribe. It's more of a reward.

Sofia's Dad: I'm a teacher as well as a parent. I know that most research says paying for grades doesn't work. It has short-term gain but long-term pain. It will backfire on your love for a subject, your internal motivation, and your creativity. That love of learning goes away, and instead what you end up loving is cash and not the subject of the learning.

Sofia: But I get an allowance for chores. What's the difference?

(Morgan's Mom and Dad enter.)
Morgan's Mom: I admit, it would be best if all children (and adults) could be motivated by an innate drive for high achievement and a thirst for knowledge. But I also believe that it's easier to accomplish good grades after getting them.

Morgan's Dad: "Fake it until you make it," I always say. The excitement and adrenaline of success are addictive, and if you get to experience it, whatever the motivation, you're inclined to seek it again.

(Alfie Kohn enters.)
Alfie Kohn: Rewards and punishments are both ways of manipulating behavior. They are two forms of doing things *to* students. And to that extent, all the research says it's counterproductive to say to students, "Do this, or here is what I'm going to do to you." This also applies to saying, "Do this, and you'll get that."

Everyone *(except Alfie Kohn)*: American author and lecturer Alfie Kohn????!!!

Alfie Kohn: In person. I truly believe that by paying kids for good grades, we are punishing them with rewards.

Morgan's Dad: I don't see a problem with offering an incentive at the end of a grading period. It's actually very similar to adult life in the career market. At the end of an evaluation period, there is an incentive to earn high marks—a promotion, a raise, or the threat of failing and losing your job.

Alfie Kohn: Clearly, this is a topic we will continue to talk about. But I have something very important to ask . . .

Morgan: What's that?

Alfie Kohn: Are you going to finish those fries?

THINK ABOUT IT
Which character in this play do you think feels most like you do on this issue? What in particular made you choose this character?

MOTIVATIONAL WORDS

Complete the concept web. Choose words and phrases at the bottom of the page to include in the web. Start with the main idea in the center circle. Then place the supporting details around the main idea. Add other circles and write words and phrases that connect to the supporting details.

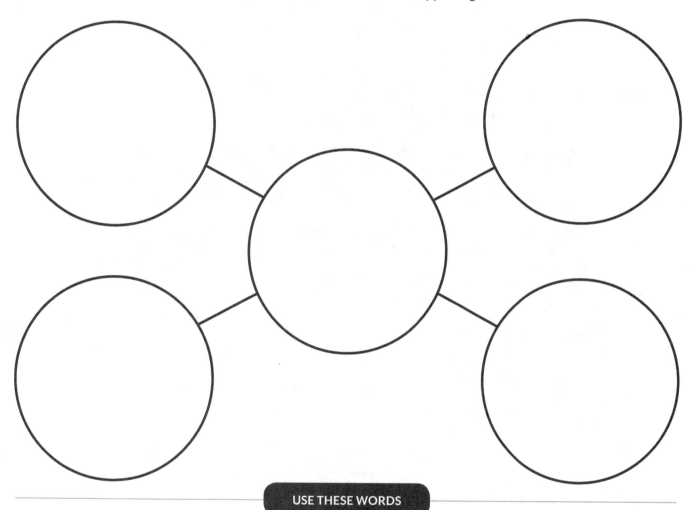

USE THESE WORDS

- independent learners
- special dinner
- fun activity
- money
- self-motivated performers
- love of learning
- short-term gain

- pride
- allowance for chores
- value education
- bribe
- reward
- motivation for working harder

- excitement of experiencing success
- manipulating behavior
- punished by rewards
- promotions at work
- a raise in pay at work

MULTIPLE PERSPECTIVES ON HOMEWORK

People have debated the subject of homework for many years. Some feel that homework helps students master material more quickly. Others think it is busy work and a waste of time. Let's examine some different perspectives on the homework debate.

TEXTS

Homework: Enough or Too Much?

This article suggests that, despite guidelines, students are receiving more homework than they should.

How much homework is too much? A recent study has found that students are getting much more homework now than in the past. Some are even getting more homework than experts recommend. In fact, some students are getting as much as three times more than what is recommended for their age!

Organizations such as the National Education Association and the National Parent-Teacher Association have something called the "10-Minute Rule." This rule states that kids should have 10 minutes of homework for whatever grade they are in. For example, first graders should have 10 minutes of homework; second graders should have 20 minutes of homework; and so on. Recently, though, researchers have found that some first graders are getting about 28 minutes of homework. And kindergartners, who are not even recommended to have homework, are getting up to 25 minutes of homework a night. "It is absolutely shocking to me to find out that particularly kindergarten students (who) are not supposed to have any homework at all . . . are getting as much homework as a third-grader is supposed to get," said Stephanie Donaldson-Pressman, the contributing editor of the study and clinical director of the New England Center for Pediatric Psychology.

But are there academic benefits to homework? In other words, does homework help kids do better in school? Here, the results are more complicated.

Some studies have shown a connection between homework and good grades, but the results were more significant in secondary school rather than in elementary school. Other studies have shown a link between homework and success on standardized tests. Other studies have found no connection at all.

Some types of homework have proven to be more beneficial than others. For example, research regarding reading at home and good grades has shown that the more kids read at home, the better they do in reading classes in school. In one study, 53 fifth-grade students kept logs of free-time activities for 8 weeks, and in a second study, 105 children kept logs for 26 weeks. The researchers compared the amount of student reading with their scores on achievement tests. The more students read outside of school, the higher they scored on reading achievement tests.

So, how much homework should kids have—a lot, a little, or none at all? Clearly, there is more homework to be done in the debate on homework!

THINK ABOUT IT

Why might teachers give homework to kindergartners? Why might teachers give more homework than is recommended?

Parents' Perspective on Homework

People often think the issue of homework only affects students and teachers. Parents are affected by homework, too. Here is an imaginary telephone conversation between two parents.

(*Telephone rings.*)

Peg: Hello?

Luis: Hi, Peg!

Peg (*wearily*): Oh, hi, Luis.

Luis: What's up? You sound miserable.

Peg: Sorry, Luis. I'm just in the middle of helping Amanda with her homework. It's the worst part of our night.

Luis: I know what you mean. Luckily, Jamie only had a little bit tonight.

Peg: I just wonder if teachers realize how hard it is on parents when they give kids homework.

Luis: I know. Lots of time, it's more work for the parents than the kids!

Peg: I mean, I understand reading every night. That's fun, and Amanda and I can sit down and do that together. It's enjoyable. But the math! Both of us are practically in tears every night!

Luis: For us, it's the opposite. It's like pulling teeth to get Jamie to read at night. It's a constant struggle. I like that the kids are made to practice their math each night. I really think it helps. I'd rather it come from the teacher than me having to assign the practice! That wouldn't go over so well.

Peg: I may have to set up a meeting with Amanda's teacher to talk about this. I'm just really torn about what to do. Maybe they could alternate nights for reading and math?

Luis: Hmmm . . . you know, I wonder if the teachers even have a say in this. They may be told by their principal or even the superintendent that they have to assign math and reading homework every night.

Peg: I hadn't thought of that.

Luis: Well, listen, I just called to let you know I'll pick up Amanda and Jamie after school tomorrow. Jamie's 30 minutes of reading is almost done. I have to make sure that kid of mine doesn't try to cut out early!

Peg (*laughs*): It's tough being us! I'll talk to you soon.

Luis: Bye, Peg!

Peg: Bye!

THINK ABOUT IT

You're a parent who likes the idea of homework. What arguments could you make?

A Student's Perspective on Homework

Here a student makes his case for getting rid of homework. He writes a persuasive letter to his teacher to try to get her to see his point of view.

January 8

Dear Mrs. Allen,

I am sorry I did not do my homework again last night. I know this is not the first time this has happened, but I've spoken to several of my friends, and we have some concerns. We wish teachers could understand that kids have a lot of other things going on in our lives other than school. We work all during the school day, which is long enough. We hardly get enough time for recess! Why should we have to do even more schoolwork when we get home?

I don't think teachers realize the pressure that is on kids these days. We are expected to be "well-rounded." That means we need to participate in after-school activities, like sports or clubs. By the time we get home from those activities, we're tired! We need to have dinner and get to bed at a "reasonable hour." How can we squeeze homework in there? We would have to make a choice—either not participate in activities that interest us, get to bed late, gobble down dinner so we can do homework, or miss doing our homework and get in trouble.

Besides doing a planned after-school activity, kids just need time to relax. Even if that means playing a video game or watching TV, it's still down time. After all, we are just kids! We will have plenty of time to work hard all day and get stressed out when we are adults. Teachers should just let kids have fun while they still can.

Times are different now. Many moms have full-time jobs outside of taking care of us kids and our homes. Sometimes an older kid needs to watch a younger brother or sister until a parent gets home. This is a big responsibility. The younger ones need a snack after school, and the older kids have to watch them to make sure nothing bad happens. How can kids take on this important responsibility when they also have homework hanging over their heads?

Please, Mrs. Allen, we promise to work hard in school all day if you will just cut out the homework. School takes up most of our weekday hours. That must be enough time for us to do what we have to do. We need a break!

THINK ABOUT IT
Which reason that Evan gives is the most convincing? Explain why.

Sincerely,

Evan Garza

Your student

A Teacher's Perspective on Homework

Here's what a teacher said during a school's Open House Night to explain his feelings about homework.

"Good evening, families and friends! Welcome to Open House Night. I am excited to talk to you about what your children will be learning this year. But before I do, I just want to talk a bit about homework. Every year, there are times when students do not hand in their homework. I wish I could make them understand how important it is. I am not giving homework to punish them. I realize that children need free time. But there are so many good things about homework.

First of all, there is a lot of research that says children who read every night get better grades in school and on state tests. The more students read, the more their vocabulary increases and the more they learn. Yes, students get time in school to read. But nothing is better than a cozy spot at home where a student can curl up with a good book. And at home, there are no school distractions, such as announcements, other students, or needing to move on to another class or activity.

Now, let's think about math for a minute. There are so many math concepts students need to understand. I teach a concept in class, students practice it a bit, then we move on. In fact, we often have to move onto another concept before students have fully mastered the one I just taught. Homework gives kids the chance to get more practice with those math skills. There are so few hours in the school day and so many skills to cover. Practicing at home helps make those concepts very clear. It also helps students remember that information when testing time comes around.

I know for students a school day can seem like forever. But there is so much to get done and not enough time in which to do it. Homework gives students the chance to complete topics and units more quickly. It helps us fit in all the learning we must cover for the year. For example, we may begin learning about colonial times in class, but we might not get to finish the reading. Or, students may not have enough time to complete their research. Students can take that work home and have it completed by the next day. That way, we can keep moving at a good pace and not fall behind in the required curriculum.

Parents and friends, I know there are things your child would rather be doing when they get home from school than homework. But it is really important they do their required assignments each night to reach their full potential this year. I will need your assistance this year in helping your children be the best they can be!"

THINK ABOUT IT

You're a parent at this Open House. What do you think about this speech?

Should Parents Help Kids With Homework?

Sometimes whether you have homework is not the only issue. If you do have homework, how much help, if any, should you get from parents or other caregivers? This article explores that question.

Eleven-year-old Emily had been stressed for days about her school project: a PowerPoint presentation on the life of J. K. Rowling. Busy with swim-team practices and religious school, she had barely had time to work on it. So she was grateful when, the night before it was due, her dad swooped in to save her.

"He said he was just going to help a little bit," Emily says. Three hours later, Emily's dad had created a dazzling work of art.

Emily got an A.

Her dad was just doing what many dedicated parents do every night, right? Whether it's correcting long-division problems, giving hints on vocabulary worksheets, or "proofing" big projects like Emily's, many parents feel it is their duty to help their children with schoolwork. And it's easy to see why kids need the help.

In most U.S. schools, homework has become more demanding and time-consuming. Studies show that many kids are stressed over school and feel more pressure than ever to do well. Between travel teams, music lessons, and other activities, some kids barely have time to eat, let alone do an hour or more of homework per night. No wonder homework often turns into a team effort between kids and parents.

But could all of this helping actually be hurting kids? Many experts say yes, especially when parents cross the line between helping and *doing*. Pointing out math mistakes is fine—unless a mom then reveals the right answers. Proofing a project is helpful, unless a father takes over. (Hear us, Emily's dad?)

Practice Makes Perfect

"I give homework for students to practice what they have learned," says fourth-grade teacher Maura Sackett. Many educators agree that if students can't do the homework, then they should let the teacher know so they can get the extra help they need. Plus, part of growing up is learning to balance outside activities and the demands of schoolwork.

A recent study by two university professors, called *The Broken Compass: Parental Involvement With Children's Education*, found that kids who got extensive homework help from their parents actually scored *worse* on standardized tests than kids who managed homework on their own.

So what's the answer to this difficult problem?

Maybe you should ask your parents—or maybe not!

THINK ABOUT IT
What is your opinion on outside homework help?

TAKE THE OTHER SIDE

Stretch your thinking. Write an essay (or a speech or letter) from the perspective you do <u>not</u> agree with— teacher, student, or parent. Put aside your personal feelings and find evidence in the texts to make a convincing argument. Complete the chart to help organize your evidence.

Who?	Perspective?	Evidence?

 10 MUST-HAVE TEXT SETS © Carol Pugliano-Martin, Scholastic Inc.

TEXT SET

3

Kids and School

YEAR-ROUND SCHOOL

When most kids hear the term "year-round school," you can see looks of horror on their faces. Parents and teachers may feel the same way. But, as with every issue, knowing all the facts can help you make a more informed decision. The following texts give you plenty of information about this issue.

TEXTS

A President's Point of View on the School Year

Read about how President Obama felt about year-round school and how the issue affects others.

In September 2010, President Obama gave a message to students and teachers. He said that the school year should be longer. Obama made it clear that he thinks American students were falling behind students in other countries, especially in math and science. He said that's got to change. He argued that the future of the country is at stake. "Whether jobs are created here, high-end jobs that support families and support the future of the American people, is going to depend on whether or not we can do something about these schools." Obama was referring to schools that were not performing well.

Most U.S. schools are in session for 180 instruction days a year, according to the Education Commission of the States. In other countries with the best achievement records, like Japan, South Korea, Germany, and New Zealand, children in lower grades are in school 197 days. Students in upper grades are in school for 196 days. That means students are in school for about one more month than American students. "That month makes a difference," Obama said. "It means that kids are losing a lot of what they learn during the school year during the summer. It's especially severe for poorer kids who may not see as many books in the house during the summers, aren't getting as many educational opportunities."

President Obama's ability to achieve his goal of longer school years was limited. States set the minimum length of school years, and there hasn't been much change in recent years. One issue is money. Obama thought that any money that went toward longer school years would be "money well spent." But it might still be hard for school districts to afford it. "It comes down to the old bugaboo, resources," said Mayor Scott Smith of Mesa, Arizona. "Everyone believes we can achieve greater things if we have a longer school year. The question is how do you pay for it?"

In Kansas, parents have resisted efforts by local school districts to extend the school year, said state education commissioner Diane DeBacker. "It's been tried," she said. She described one instance of a Topeka-area elementary school that got rid of year-round schooling after just one year. "The community was just not ready for kids to be in school all summer long. Kids wanted to go swimming. Their families wanted to go on vacation."

Clearly, the issue of year-round school is still up in the air. It will be interesting to see how future presidents feel about this controversial topic.

THINK ABOUT IT
Without year-round school, how else could students make up lost classroom time in the summer?

The Board of Ed Meeting

This play takes place at a Board of Education meeting. Parents, teachers, administrators, and students have come to get the facts about year-round schooling. You will discover that there are different points of view on the subject. Perhaps you and your fellow students can vote on the issue after the play!

Characters:

Ms. Ruiz, Board of Education President

Professor Bennett

Mrs. Sherwin, Principal

Mr. Reilly, Teacher

Mr. Verdi, Parent

Samantha, Student

Scene: Board of Education Meeting at Rail Valley Elementary School, September

Ms. Ruiz: Thank you all for being here tonight. This is a great turnout, so I guess our topic of discussion is of interest to many people. The topic of year-round school has been talked about and debated for several years now in the Rail Valley School District. Tonight we will hear the different perspectives surrounding this issue and then take a vote on what is the best for our district. We are lucky to have a special guest here with us to present his research before we open the floor up for comments and questions. Please welcome Professor Martin Bennett from the Educational Studies Department at Rail Valley Community College. Professor Bennett, perhaps you can begin by telling us what year-round school is.

Professor Bennett: Contrary to what many people think when they hear about it, year-round school does not mean students are in school non-stop for the whole year. Students still go to school for a total of 180 days a year, just like they do in non-year-round schools. But instead of having one long summer break, the same 180 days of school are divided into 9-week quarters. After each quarter, there is a three-week break in fall, winter, and spring. There's also about a month off for summer.

Ms. Ruiz: I think that clears things up for a lot of people, thank you. Now, you've researched this topic for many years. What can you tell us about its worth to students?

Professor Bennett: Well, it is true that kids forget much of what they've learned during a school year after the summer months. But we just don't know if year-round school increases students' performance on standardized tests. It can be helpful, though, to lower-income students, children with learning disabilities, and those for whom English is a second language. Basically, year-round school <u>may</u> improve children's learning. But what's most important is what they do when they're in school.

Ms. Ruiz: Thank you, Professor Bennett. Now I will open up the floor to the principals, teachers, parents, and students in our audience. Mrs. Sherwin, you'd like to speak?

Mrs. Sherwin: Yes, thank you. Hello, everyone. Most of you know me. I'm Mrs. Sherwin, Principal at Rail Elementary. I am very much in support of the year-round model. I have spoken with principals in other school districts, and they say students have much more energy after frequent breaks from school. They pack a lot of learning into the nine-week sessions. After that time, they are ready for a break. After the break, they are ready to go to work again.

Continued on next page >>

Mr. Reilly: I understand what Mrs. Sherwin is saying about kids enjoying frequent breaks, but all I can think about is how disruptive the schedule would be for teachers and students. Once we get a good momentum going with our studies, we would have to go on a break. When we return, it would be very hard for everyone to get motivated again.

Ms. Ruiz: You all know Mr. Reilly, one of our third-grade teachers here at Rail. Can you explain what you mean, Mr. Reilly?

Mr. Reilly: Well, I have enough trouble keeping my students focused every day on what they are required to learn. With holidays, friends, sports, and other things on their minds, it's difficult enough to get them to concentrate on their schoolwork. But if there were so many vacations to look forward to, well, I just don't think I can compete with that! *(Everyone laughs.)*

Ms. Ruiz: Mr. Verdi? Your daughter is in fourth grade at Rail Elementary. Do you have something to add?

Mr. Verdi: Yes. We moved here recently from another school district. That district had the year-round schedule. That is why we moved. The schedule was a nightmare for finding childcare for Samantha. In the summer, there are many programs and camps to choose from. But with this proposal, we'd have to find a baby-sitter every few months for several weeks. It would be a real financial burden.

Samantha: It makes playing sports difficult, too. I play soccer and if other schools are on a regular school schedule, we may not have any teams to play. We would be in school while they are on vacation and the other way around.

Ms. Ruiz: I thank you all very much for your input on this issue. Clearly there are many things to consider as we decide whether or not the Rail Valley School District will make the change to year-round school. I think we're ready to have a vote. Let's begin.

THINK ABOUT IT
What would your vote be at the end of this meeting? Explain why.

Cedar Rapids Year-Round Elementary School Credits Success to Its Calendar

This transcript of a KCRG-TV news report from July 20, 2015, tells about a year-round school success story.

A Cedar Rapids elementary school opened its doors this morning for the 126th time holding its first day of school. Taylor Elementary School operates year-round with shorter but more frequent breaks in between classes. Taylor is one of the lowest income schools in the city. In the 2013–2014 school year, 87.6 percent of students received free or reduced lunch.

Parents say their kids might have some mixed feelings about having class in July. Gilda McCleary, a Taylor Elementary parent, says, "As a kid I'm like, ugh, year-round school? That stinks! But as a parent now, as an adult, I really like it. [Students] don't lose as much."

And the kids like it, too. Fifth-grade student Sydney Murrz says, "It is awesome because I get to get out earlier than other schools." Amilee Lamere, also in fifth grade, agrees. "We have different teachers and staff, and we learn more than other schools."

Principal Brian Christoffersen says there are some great benefits behind staying connected. "Kids are being socially-connected in school with their friends. And they have caring adult relationships with their teachers and two healthy meals every day. When you think about it, it's the 21st century, and we shut down all learning for three consecutive months. It just really doesn't make a lot of sense."

Christoffersen says there are a lot of factors behind test scores, but he thinks the calendar is helping. "At least for the past four years, we've experienced growth every single year in our state test scores," says Christoffersen. "So I'd like to think it makes a difference."

Christoffersen says breaking up that long summer break and making shorter, two- or three-week breaks more frequently gives students a chance to recharge and come back fresh.

THINK ABOUT IT

Were you surprised by any of the students' reactions to year-round school? Why? Can you think of any other benefits of this program?

Debate: Should School Be Year-Round?

Two *Scholastic News* readers weigh in on the year-round school debate.

Most students can look forward to having a couple of months off during the summer. But some students attend one of nearly 3,000 year-round schools in the U.S. These schools are in session the same number of days as other schools. But instead of a long summer vacation, they take a few two- to four-week breaks throughout the year. Workers at these schools say students can learn more without long breaks in class time. With shorter breaks, teachers spend less time reviewing material when students return to school.

But people who believe in longer breaks say students at year-round school miss out on fun activities, like summer camps. They also argue that these schools spend more on air-conditioning and other expenses.

Here's what two of our readers think.

Yes: Patrick Hallisey, Pennsylvania

Students should go to school year-round. During the summer, I forget some things I've learned during the school year. At year-round schools, teachers don't have to spend as much time reviewing information when school picks up after a break. Year-round schools also have more-frequent vacation breaks, so you'd get more chances to have fun with your friends outside of school.

No: Zippy Lichoro, Iowa

Students should not go to school year-round. Having a long summer break is important for both students and teachers. Having school year-round would be unfair to people who want to take long summer trips. Also, summer is a great time for kids to play outside because the weather is warm. It's better to have a long summer vacation than shorter breaks when the weather might not be as nice.

THINK ABOUT IT

Put aside your personal opinion. Which student makes the better case? Why do you think so?

BALANCE THE ISSUE

Which side of the issue of year-round schools has more weight? Write all the pros you have read about and can think of on the left side of the scale. Write all of the cons you have read about and can think of on the right side of the scale. If this scale could move, which side would be heavier? Tell a partner why.

Can you tip the scale on year-round school?

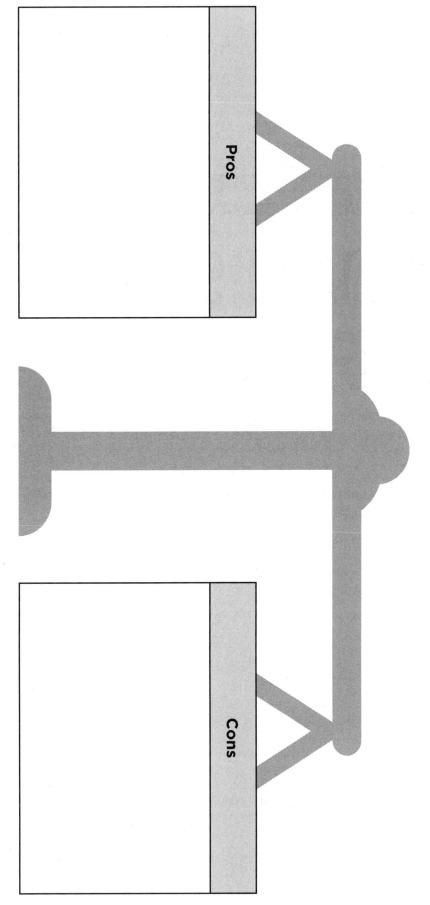

Pros

Cons

ANIMALS IN CAPTIVITY

You may have read about the question of whether zoos are positive or negative. Some of these texts are slightly different. This set contains not only articles presenting different points of view, but also an editorial cartoon and a link to a video clip of famous animal scientist Jane Goodall.

TEXTS

A Tale of Two Zoo Animals

This article tells the story of two animals in captivity. One is Gus, the polar bear who lived in New York City. The other is Maggie, the elephant who was moved from Alaska to California.

Gus the polar bear was a local celebrity in New York City. The star of the Central Park Zoo, Gus was visited by more than 20 million people. He arrived at the zoo in 1988. People marveled at the sight of an animal most people would never get the chance to see in the wild. But in 1994, zookeepers began noticing Gus behaving strangely. He would swim back and forth in his pool in the same patterns for up to 12 hours each day. Animal experts were hired to determine how to help Gus. Some decided that Gus was bored. Animals in the wild spend much of their time hunting for food. Because Gus was given all of his meals by the zookeepers, he did not have that activity to keep him occupied, and he did not know what else to do with himself.

Experts came up with activities to keep Gus's mind busy. They hid food in toys so that Gus would have to work to get it. Gus also took medicine to help him with his problem. The constant swimming declined a bit, but Gus never seemed to be completely content. The deaths of his female polar bear partners also took their toll on Gus. He died in 2013, having lived longer than most polar bears in captivity, who live an average of 21 years.

Today, many people think it was unfair to have Gus living in a small zoo enclosure. They claim Gus's behavior was a result of being a victim of captivity and polar bears and other wild animals belong in the wild, not in zoos.

Maggie the elephant suffered a similar fate. She was in the Alaska Zoo after her herd in Africa had been culled (the process of killing several elephants in a herd to control the population). Maggie was one year old in 1983, when she arrived in Alaska. She had another elephant, Annabelle, to keep her company. But when Annabelle died in 1997, Maggie lived alone in a small, outdoor pen with a shallow pond in the summer and in a small enclosure with an unheated floor during the winter. The zoo made her a treadmill so that she could get exercise, but Maggie did not use it. One day, zoo workers found Maggie lying on her side, unable to get up. It took workers 19 hours to get her standing again. Two days later, the same thing happened. Many people in Alaska started a campaign to get Maggie moved to a warmer place with more room for her to roam and other elephants for her to interact with. In 2007, Maggie was moved to an elephant sanctuary in California, where she is doing very well.

THINK ABOUT IT

Do you think workers did enough for Gus and Maggie? If so, why? If not, what more could they have done?

Jane Goodall Speaks About Chimpanzees in Zoos

BY ERIC BERGER

Jane Goodall is a scientist who has studied chimpanzees her whole life. This excerpt was taken from an interview with her on February 20, 2011.

Question: Do you support chimpanzees in zoos, or is that something you'd rather not see?

Jane Goodall: It depends on the zoo. I've just been getting horror reports on some chimpanzees in third-world zoos that make me shiver. But there are still roadside zoos in the United States that make me shiver. Quite honestly, when people ask me, I say to think about the various situations in which chimpanzees could live. It can be the best of all places in the wild that are protected, like Gombe. Then there are lots of other wilderness areas. But unless the chimps are lucky and in a faraway place, their forests are going to be disturbed by people cutting them down for timber or to move in. Also, they can be hunted, as they are across large areas of Africa. So you might not want to be there.

At the other end of the extreme, there are five-foot-by-five-foot cages in medical research labs in very modern countries, including the United States. There are also very bad zoos and circuses. Then you get the really good zoos, which have large enclosed areas, with enriched environments and a group of chimps together, keepers who love them and understand them, and an adoring public. Then I say, suppose you were a chimp—and that's

▶ **For more on Jane Goodall's viewpoints on zoos, watch the following video:**
http://www.youtube.com/watch?v=w9eqh_kGg-Q

what some of these animal-rights people can't get their minds around—it's what they think is best for the chimp. I want people to think about what the chimp would prefer. So if you're a chimp, your best choices may be to be in a secure place in the wild or in a really good zoo. None of the other options are really of any use. This kind of idea that any kind of wild is always good is not right.

THINK ABOUT IT

Do you think we can really imagine what it is like to be a chimp or another animal? Explain your answer.

Excerpted and adapted from "Jane Goodall on why zoos are sometimes better than the wild, and much more." Retrieved March 17, 2016, from Chron http://blog.chron.com/sciguy/2011/02/jane-goodall-on-why-zoos-are-sometimes-better-than-the-wild-and-much-more/. Used by permission.

National Zoo

Cartoons often appear on the op-ed (opinion-editorial) pages of a newspaper.

In the cartoon below, the artist presents a definite point of view.

THINK ABOUT IT

What opinion do you think is being expressed in this cartoon? What evidence do you have for your answer?

It's a Boy! And a Girl!

Conservation is an aspect of zoos many people don't know about. This news release celebrates the birth of two bison calves. Bison were once in danger of extinction.

Officials at the Chicago Zoological Society, which manages Brookfield Zoo, are happy to announce the recent births of two bison calves! One was a male who was born in May of 2014. Another was a female born in June of the same year.

But why all the fuss over a couple of bison calves? First of all, a bison calf has not been born in the zoo since 2012. But, most important, bison are one of the first conservation success stories in North America. Long ago, millions of bison roamed the Great Plains. But as new settlers moved out west, almost all of the bison were killed for their meat, bones, and hides. By the end of the 19th century, there were fewer than 1,000 bison left.

Today, bison are making a comeback. Approximately 500,000 live on ranches and tribal lands. About 20,000 live in protected parks and preserves such as Yellowstone National Park. Additionally, another conservation organization, called American Prairie Foundation, is working with government and other conservation organizations to increase bison populations by protecting the animals and their habitat. The organization is purchasing private land so that bison may roam freely once again. In partnership with the World Wildlife Fund, American Prairie Foundation is putting together a multimillion-acre wildlife reserve to protect the grassland of northeastern Montana, where bison and other wildlife can thrive.

Many zoos and conservation organizations are connected in the United States. They work together to help keep different species of animals from becoming extinct. They do this through what is called a "captive breeding program." Some animals will remain at the zoo while others will live in wildlife refuges.

THINK ABOUT IT

Should we try to stop animal species from going extinct? Or is extinction a part of nature? Explain your answer.

Zoos Can Be Better for Wild Animals Than the Wild

BY RUTH PADEL

Is the wild too wild for animals? This article suggests that zoos are a good alternative.

Some people argue that wild animals belong in the wild. But their wild homes are vanishing, so what's a wild animal to do? Many people think zoos are the answer. The aim of good zoos today is conservation.

Most zoo animals are born in zoos. The days of capturing them from the wild are long gone. Zoos breed wild animals. Most animals that have been born in zoos would not know how to survive in the wild. They wouldn't know how to protect themselves from predators or how to hunt for food. Having these animals in zoos allows them to teach others about their wild relatives and to persuade people to take measures to care for them and their habitat.

Since the 1970s, wild animals' habitats have disappeared. Responsible zoos have become places of education and science whose prime concern is conserving the wild. The animals live in the social groups and habitats they like.

Because of us, zoos are sometimes the only way nature has to survive in our world now. Many animals have lost their homes to plantations, mines, and fields used to make goods for humans.

The wild can be a dangerous place for animals. Habitat destruction and poaching are wiping out whole species of wild animals. Scientists can learn from zoo animals about how to protect their wild cousins better.

Many children suffer from something some people call "nature-deficit disorder." They have never been away from their city environment. There is nothing like seeing an inner-city child look at a wild animal for the first time.

To survive, wild nature needs future generations to care about conservation. Zoo animals can make millions of people aware that these creatures are real and need help. Every time someone pays to visit a zoo run by a conservation organization, he or she helps to protect the animals' endangered cousins.

THINK ABOUT IT
Even though zoos help people appreciate animals, should we keep animals in zoos? Use evidence from this text set to support your answer.

Adapted from "Don't Let Good Zoos Go Extinct" by Ruth Padel, *The Guardian*, March 22, 2013. Copyright © 2013 by The Guardian. Used by permission.

GRAPHIC ORGANIZER **Name** ____________________ **Date** ____________

ZOOS VS. THE WILD

Use these T-charts to organize the information you learned about animals in zoos and animals in the wild.

Zoos	
Pros	**Cons**

Wild	
Pros	**Cons**

Now, put it all together. What general statement can you make about this issue? Include all the perspectives.

____

____

____

____

____

____

____

E-BOOKS OR PRINT BOOKS?

As I compiled this section, I wondered if electronic books would still be popular after this book was published. Then I realized the issue is broader than that. There will always be a need to be well informed about facts in order to weigh the pros and cons of an issue. We should also be mindful of people's feelings about change. This set uses articles as well as personal opinions to get to the heart of the electronic books vs. print books debate.

TEXTS

E-Books vs. Print: What Parents Need to Know

BY JENNY DEAM

Parents and child experts are particularly torn over this issue. What is best for children?

When Maggie Moore, a suburban Denver mom, was packing for a family trip, she was stumped by her 4-year-old son's stack of favorite books. He had dozens, and she knew they'd be too heavy to take along. But they would be away for a few weeks — how could she bring only a few?

That's when she reluctantly bought an e-reader, loading titles for both of them onto it. What happened next surprised her: From the moment her son held the device and began to scroll through a book, he was transfixed. "He was in heaven," says Moore.

E-reading devices have been around only a few years, but it's already hard to imagine life without them. And like all things tech, what started as a product for adults is now targeted at a younger audience. In fact, according to Scholastic's *Kids & Family Reading Report*, the percentage of children who have read an e-book has almost doubled since 2010, jumping to 46 percent. And e-books for kids and teens became the fastest-growing segment in 2011, according to the Association of American Publishers and the Book Industry Study Group.

"We are not going to stop this train," says psychologist Jim Taylor, Ph.D., author of *Raising Generation Tech*. But should we try to slow it down? When it comes to the youngest readers, some experts are skittish about putting tablets into tiny hands. Parents are conflicted, too — 68 percent prefer that their 6- to 8-year-olds read print books, Scholastic found. Since there's not much research out there, it may be years before we understand the impact of tech devices on young readers.

Still, there are signs that e-readers can have a positive effect on newbie readers, especially when it comes to targeted learning based on each child's ability. But don't give those storybooks the heave-ho just yet. "It doesn't have to be an either-or. You don't build a house with only one tool," says Otis Kriegel, a fifth-grade teacher in New York City and the author of *Covered in Glue: What New Elementary School Teachers Really Need to Know*.

THINK ABOUT IT

Should libraries provide e-books for people to check out? Should schools have e-books for students to borrow? How do you think publishing companies feel about this? Support your answers.

Excerpted and adapted from "Reading Revolution," *Scholastic Parent & Child*, February/March 2013. Copyright © by Scholastic Inc. Reprinted by permission.

Different Voices

The issue of e-books versus print books affects different kinds of people. Here are the views of teachers, a librarian, and fans of both print books and e-books.

Teacher #1

E-readers are amazing tools for kids—giving them the world of literature at their fingertips! With e-readers, you can take notes, highlight, and bookmark. These are things you cannot do with library books. You always have a dictionary within your reach. You can tap on the word and get the definition. This makes e-readers worth their weight in gold. Also, some e-readers have access to the Internet, so if students are reading a historical piece and want more information on a person or event right away, it's there. This can help my students' understanding of what they're reading. They have a better frame of reference. We don't need encyclopedias! And that text-to-speech feature is great. It reads the text aloud. It really helps ELL children or other kids who may struggle with reading. They can listen to the text until they are comfortable reading on their own.

Teacher #2

I'd rather see kids holding a book in their hands. All kids do nowadays is stare at screens. I want them to open a book and turn the pages. Stop staring at a screen and go to the library where you see that other people also like to read. I want them to have an actual conversation with someone in that library (or bookstore) about the book they are reading. I get e-readers. I just don't think they should come at the expense of actual books, especially for students. Kids cannot use sticky notes or mark up e-readers.

That's a big part of our reading curriculum. If students have a dictionary at their fingertips, they won't learn how to use context clues. Some may ask, "Isn't that an antiquated skill?" Not when it comes to having a conversation, it isn't! You can't consult your online dictionary while you're in the middle of talking with someone. And as for the text-to-speech feature, how can a computer voice compare with a human voice? One more thing: Are kids going to get bullied in school because some have the latest, greatest tablet while others may have a very inexpensive tablet because that's all their parents can afford? Food for thought.

Librarian

E-books? Why would anyone need me anymore? Without print books, I would lose my job and so would many others. Every day when I walk into work, I breathe in the smell of the books on the shelves. It always makes me feel better. I love meeting the patrons who come in looking for a book. I pride myself in knowing a great many titles, and I've read much of what we have in our stacks. There's nothing

Continued on next page >>

like having the challenge of matching people with the perfect books. And then to have them come back to tell me how much they loved those books. There's nothing better. Without print books, we'll lose so much human connection. And if you ask me, that's one thing we really can't afford to lose.

E-book Fan

I love them! Travel-wise, they are lightweight, and you can access more than one book at a time. You can check out five library books at a time from your couch. There is really no reason for print books anymore, as much as I love them. I think eventually print books will go away. We'll look back on this time in history as life-changing. We've had computers, cell phones, etc. Someday, these technologies will seem as old as paper and ink or the printing press. It's a shift in thinking. You can't just hold on to the idea of a print book because you like the way it feels. You can access a book from multiple devices—your tablet, e-reader, and even your phone. No more, "Oops! I forgot my book!" You usually have your phone with you, so you can read anytime, anywhere! I haven't read a print book since I got my e-reader. But you'll find people split down the middle—it's black or white, no gray in the middle. For some, part of the enjoyment of reading is actually holding the book, turning the pages, the way it smells. For me, it's only about the words, which is why I just love my e-reader. You don't get dirty hands from the ink. Also, I prefer adjusting the size of the text with my e-reader to wearing reading glasses with a book! E-reader or print book? No competition. E-readers win: compact, clean, touch a button and download a book that's cheaper than paper, and doesn't kill trees. Words are words. An electronic interface doesn't change that.

Print-book Fan

I'm old-fashioned. I love the feel of the actual book in my hands, especially a great one where you turn the pages with excitement, anticipation. That's lost with technology. Everyone speaks about e-readers on the beach. Can't you drop it and ruin it? With a book, you just shake the sand off. I also love the sight of bookshelves in my home. And don't get me started about highlighting the passages you love! It's so much fun to do. It's almost like using a coloring book, but you are coloring great words! I have a tablet, and I use it more as a vacation PC substitute. I like "real" books! I love seeing my bookmark move deeper and deeper into a good book. To put it simply: Book in my hands, sand in my toes, there's nothing like a real book!

> **THINK ABOUT IT**
> What are the purposes of reading? Which format best suits those purposes? Does each format serve a different purpose?

A Discovery in the Future

This play, which takes place in the future, shows what might happen if archaeologists discover a book at a dig site.

Characters:
Sam, an archaeologist
Hank, Sam's boss

Time: 2214 (or later)

Place: Anytown, USA

Scene: Two archaeologists are digging at a site.

Sam: Boss, look! I think I've found something!

Hank: What is it?

Sam: It's hard to tell. It's very delicate. I'm afraid to move it too much.

Hank: Let me see. Hmmm . . . This is a very thin material. It's almost transparent. And there are words on it. Sam, I think you've discovered a book!

Sam: A book? Wow! I learned about them in college, but I've never actually seen one!

Hank: Well, here is one! As you know, people used to read them. They were made of paper and printed on with ink.

Sam: Paper and ink. Such ancient materials!

Hank: You may have also learned that books were a very big industry. There were whole stores devoted to selling just books. There were even places called "libraries" where people could borrow books, read them, and then return them.

Sam: That's so cute. It's sharing! But people must have been so excited to replace their books with electronic readers.

Hank: Actually, if I remember correctly, my great-great-great grandmother told me there was a real divide when it came to books versus e-readers.

Sam: That's strange. I can't imagine anyone preferring this flimsy thing to our multi-purpose electronic devices. It is very quaint, though. Kind of like that car on wheels that we found last year.

Hank: Keep digging, Sam. There's no telling what we'll find next!

THINK ABOUT IT
What other technologies do you think will become out-of-date in the near future? How might people in the future misinterpret some of our technologies?

WANTED!
PRINT BOOKS! E-BOOKS!

Create a "Wanted!" poster for each format: print books and e-books.

Wanted! Print Books

_____

_____

_____

_____

_____

_____

_____

Wanted! E-Books

_____

_____

_____

_____

_____

_____

_____

TEXT SET

6

Current Events

WHY EXPLORE SPACE?

"This is the new ocean and I believe the United States must sail on it and be in a position second to none."
– President John F. Kennedy, on space exploration

Many people have been thrilled watching humans explore space. But is the thrill now gone? This text set presents some of the different ways people feel about space exploration.

TEXTS

What's the Future of U.S. Space Exploration?

This transcript of a 2013 video gives background on the space program. Since the video was made, NASA has completed a few unmanned Mars missions.

▶ Watch the video:
https://www.youtube.com/watch?v=Mr7jqzq1piU

In the United States, manned space flight stopped in July of 2011, when the shuttle *Atlantis* came in for a safe landing at the Kennedy Space Center. So for the last two years, and for years to come, the United States is forced to hitch a ride to the *International Space Station* on Russian *Soyuz* flights. It's a far cry from the glory days of the space race and the effort to put a man on the moon. The most significant event in space exploration happened more than 40 years ago—*Apollo 11*'s successful lunar landing.

So where is the United States these days in the battle for the great beyond? "I put us at the top of the heap," says Michael Lopez-Alegria, a former U.S. astronaut. He believes the U.S. will need to work hard to keep its position because there are other countries that want to take our place.

With the space shuttle retired, and the next version of manned space flight, *Orion,* still years away, NASA looks to other advances, including landing a rover on Mars. But most of NASA's big plans to explore remain on paper, and so much of that depends on government funding. At around 16 to 17 billion dollars annually, paying for NASA represents about one half of one percent of the annual U.S. budget. Lopez-Alegria says, "For such a small investment, we get such great return:

inspiration, pride, technology, education, . . . jobs." The U.S. is the clear leader in privately funded space exploration. Lopez-Alegria points out that, as the past has shown, governments should do the difficult exploration and opening of frontiers, and then private companies can get involved in smaller tasks.

So while NASA shoots for Mars, Lopez-Alegria says private companies can bring payloads back and forth to the *International Space Station.* And in coming years, many companies have their sights set on space tourism. Commercial success may be the spark that brings back U.S. interest in the space program and hope that its golden years are not in the rearview mirror.

THINK ABOUT IT
When the United States explores space, is it competing with other countries? Explain your answer.

Keep the Money at Home

This author clearly feels there are more important things to spend money on than space exploration.

Why should we stop spending money on space exploration? With all that is going on in the world today, I cannot even believe this is still up for debate!

Look around you. Look at the news. There is so much poverty in the world—and not only in third-world countries! Some of the wealthiest nations still have areas of extreme poverty. Can you imagine how many people billions of dollars could feed? And it's not only food we could buy. We could build thousands of homes for homeless people.

Also, our country is trillions of dollars in debt. That means we owe tons of money to other countries. All of that space money would make a great dent in that debt.

Some may argue that we should explore space to look for another planet to colonize if something goes wrong with Earth. Well, if we spent that space money on improving conditions on Earth, we wouldn't have to look for another habitable planet!

Please write to the government and ask them to stop spending tons of money on outer space. We need the money right here at home.

THINK ABOUT IT

Do you agree with this person's opinion? If so, what points do you agree most with? If not, why do you think we should explore space?

Pluto's First Close-Up

BY SARA GOUDARZI

This 2015 article tells about a NASA space probe that recently traveled to Pluto.
The probe provided scientists with a lot of new information about the dwarf planet.

This artist's illustration shows *New Horizons* nearing Pluto on July 14, 2015.

NASA's *New Horizons* probe has been zooming toward Pluto for more than nine years. After a 3 billion-mile journey, the tiny spacecraft finally zipped by the **dwarf planet** on Tuesday. Dwarf planets are objects that **orbit** (circle) the sun but are too small to be considered planets.

On July 14, 2015, at 7:49 a.m. EDT, scientists, engineers, and others on Earth broke out in cheers as the spacecraft flew within 7,750 miles of Pluto's surface. *New Horizons* is the first probe to get so close to the dwarf planet.

"This is a tremendous moment in human history," said NASA science chief John Grunsfeld.

A HISTORIC FLYBY

Pluto was once called a planet but was later named a dwarf planet by scientists. It lies in an unexplored region of space known as the **Kuiper** (KAI-per) **belt.** This region is packed with space rocks and other mini-planets orbiting the sun. Because Pluto and its five moons are small and so far away, scientists don't know a lot about them.

Continued on next page >>

The *New Horizons* mission is helping to change that. It can fly at about 31,000 miles per hour and is the size of a piano. It is equipped with seven scientific instruments and flew by Pluto to collect data and take pictures. The probe also flew within 17,000 miles of Charon, Pluto's largest moon.

During the encounter, which lasted about 10 hours, the probe made some 900 scientific observations. These included recording temperatures around Pluto, taking measurements of its atmosphere, and mapping the dwarf planet and its moons.

CALLING HOME

Because Pluto is 3.625 billion miles away, it takes approximately 4.5 hours for spacecraft signals to reach Earth. As soon as *New Horizons* finished its data collection on the afternoon of July 14, it called home. The first signal, indicating a successful encounter with Pluto, was received back on Earth at 8:52 p.m. EDT.

Before its closest approach, *New Horizons* sent the first-ever high-resolution photo of Pluto. The spacecraft's observations showed that Pluto is about 736 miles from its center to its outside. This shows that Pluto is larger than scientists once thought. In fact, it's larger than any other object in the region. Some people now call it the king of the Kuiper belt.

Scientists also confirmed that a bright patch near the dwarf planet's north pole is an ice cap, thanks to *New Horizons'* **spectrometer**. A spectrometer is a tool that splits visible light into separate colors. That allows scientists to gather information about an object's makeup.

BEYOND PLUTO

Learning about the outskirts of our planetary neighborhood can help scientists understand the origins of our solar system and even life itself. Researchers think it's possible that cosmic dust from the outer regions of the solar system could have delivered **organic material** to our planet. Organic material is made up of special chemical compounds that contain carbon and are the building blocks of living organisms on Earth.

The probe is now heading deeper into the Kuiper belt. Scientists expect *New Horizons* to encounter hundreds of other small and icy worlds.

"The universe has a lot more variety than we thought . . . and that's wonderful," said Alan Stern, the project's principal investigator. "The most exciting discoveries will likely be the ones we don't anticipate."

THINK ABOUT IT

What would the *New Horizons* team say about why it's important to explore places such as Pluto and beyond? Use information from the text to support your answer.

Why We Explore

Bill Nye (the Science Guy), American science educator, makes his thoughts on space exploration clear.

▶ Watch the video: https://www.youtube.com/watch?v=FVZmL5UARcs

If you stop exploring . . . what does that say about you? You're not going to move forward as a species. Your country's economy will fall behind. Space exploration stimulates the economy. For me, the search for extra-terrestrial life is part of space exploration and, therefore, something you just do. Copernicus goes, "The Sun is the center, not the Earth." Everybody's like, "What? Dude! Yeah! The Earth goes around the Sun. Oh, now everything adds up." Galileo says, "Hey you know we're not the only planet with a moon." "Oh, we're going to have to put you in prison." So, if we found evidence of life elsewhere, it would humble us in the same way. There are many people that are troubled by this uncertainty and they want to have all the answers. But that's not the nature of nature, and it's not the nature of science. Science is this process where we keep making discoveries and, in general, the more discoveries you make, the more you realize you don't know. You're always going to find something—especially in space.

THINK ABOUT IT

Is exploring always a good idea? Can you think of some examples of when exploration is a bad idea?

Dreams of Space, "Why Explore Space?"

Raymond Bell, the narrator of this award-winning video, agrees with Bill Nye.

▶ Watch the video: https://www.youtube.com/watch?v=QQXd4qc-A8k

You ask me why we should explore space. Well, let me tell you a story. A young boy comes home from school one day, excited with a smile on his face, sees his dad and says, "Hey, Dad, you won't believe what I learned in school today! I learned people went to the moon! Do you think I could go to the moon?" His father looks at him and says, "I'm sorry, son. People don't do things like that anymore." The boy's smile fades away. Fighting back tears, he says, "Why? Why?" His dad says, "Sometimes you lose something and you forget how important it was. See, son, people don't dream like they used to."

So you ask me why we should explore space. Well, let me ask you—do you dream? I think people forget—this country was built on three things: blood, sweat, and the dreams of those brave enough to do so. And if we stop dreaming, what do we really have?

So, to all the believers, the broken, the fallen, the have-nots, and the might-never-bes, I have one thing to say to you—dream on.

THINK ABOUT IT

Compare the video transcript to the one on page 52. How are these two videos alike? How are they different? What is the main idea of each video?

Mars Can Wait. Oceans Can't.

BY AMITAI ETZIONI

A professor at George Washington University gives a different perspective on space exploration. Here are some excerpts from an editorial he wrote for CNN.com.

Washington (CNN) – . . . There are very good reasons to stop spending billions of dollars on manned space missions. We can explore space in ways that are safer and much less costly. We can also grant much higher priority to other scientific and engineering projects, like exploring the oceans.

The main costs of space exploration come from the fact that we send humans, rather than robots. There are several reasons why such efforts drive up the costs. A human needs a return ticket, while a robot can go one way. Space vehicles for humans must be made safe, while we can risk a bunch of robots without losing sleep. Robots are much easier to feed. They experience little trouble when subject to prolonged weightlessness. They are much easier to shield from radiation. And they can do most tasks humans can.

Meanwhile, ninety percent of the ocean floor has not even been charted. While we have been to the moon, the technology to explore the ocean's floors is still being developed.

The oceans play a major role in controlling our climate. But we have not learned yet how to use them to cool us off rather than contribute to our overheating. Ocean organisms may hold the promise of cures for many diseases. An examination of the unique eyes of skate (ray fish) led to advances in combating blindness. The horseshoe crab was crucial in developing a test for bacterial contamination.

These are just two of many important discoveries made thanks to the ocean.

Water is in danger of becoming scarce. We badly need more efficient and less costly methods to remove the salt from ocean water. By 2025, 1.8 billion people are expected to suffer from severe water scarcity. That number is expected to jump to 3.9 billion by 2050. That is well over a third of the entire global population.

If the oceans do not excite you, how about engineering a bacteria that eats carbon dioxide? This could help protect the world from overheating. It could also produce fuel, which will allow us to drive our cars and machines without oil. I am sure that people would be just as impressed or inspired with such breakthroughs as with one more set of photos of a faraway galaxy or a whole Milky Way full of stars.

In short, do not cry for Mars. It is not going away. We can send R2D2 to explore it and still keep a whole pile of money for important and inspiring exploration missions right here on Earth, starting at the beach nearest you.

THINK ABOUT IT

Which do you think is more important to explore—space or the oceans? Give evidence from this text set to support your answer.

Name _____   Date _____

SHOULD WE EXPLORE SPACE?

Complete each point of the star. Write your thoughts on each perspective in a box.

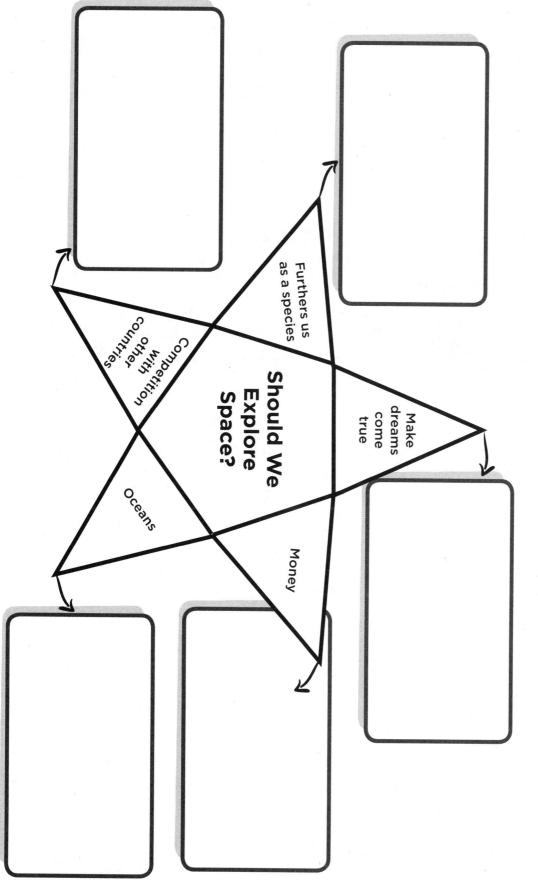

Furthers us as a species

Make dreams come true

Competition with other countries

Should We Explore Space?

Oceans

Money

THE "FIRST" THANKSGIVING

As with many historical events, there is much debate about what our so-called "first" Thanksgiving was like. Since we cannot interview anyone who was there, we can only rely on firsthand, written accounts of the event. There are only two existing primary sources, which are included in their original form and translated into modern-day English.

TEXTS

ONLINE ARTICLE

The Pilgrims Give Thanks

This text gives an overview of what we call the "First" Thanksgiving.

Ten months after their arrival at Plimoth, the Pilgrims had built seven houses, a common meeting place, and three storehouses for supplies and food from their first harvest. They had much to be thankful for after barely surviving the winter.

The Food

Having meat on your table in 1621 meant shooting it yourself. Ducks were probably the main course. Waterfowl was plentiful in the Bay area. The Pilgrim women would have roasted the freshly plucked ducks over the fire. Their children would have pitched in by grinding corn into *samp*, a kind of porridge or corn-based oatmeal.

The Pilgrims would not have survived at Plimoth without the help of the native Wampanoag people and their leader, Massasoit. So it was fitting that he and his men joined the Pilgrim's feast. (Massasoit was actually a title, meaning *Great Sachem* or leader, used by the Wampanoag chief. His birth name was Ousamequin.)

Massasoit sent several men to hunt deer as a gift to the English for their feast. Venison, or deer meat, was a favorite Wampanoag dish.

There is only one written account of the first Thanksgiving, and turkey isn't mentioned. And cranberry sauce and mashed potatoes weren't even invented yet! In addition to duck and venison, the diners likely enjoyed seafood, cabbage, onions, corn, and squash.

The Festivities

The 1621 feast was not one big sit-down meal. Meals were eaten throughout the colony, both indoors and out, for almost a week. Some meals the Wampanoag and the English ate together, and other times the two groups ate separately.

Between meals, the Pilgrims and the Wampanoag played games. The Wampanoag might have taught the English Pin Game, where a player tried to toss a small ring onto a pin. Wampanoag and Pilgrim children might have played Blind Man's Bluff together as well.

One of the grown-up sports among the English was target shooting, where men competed to see who was the best shot. Besides sports, there was also singing and dancing among both the Wampanoag and the Pilgrims.

THINK ABOUT IT

How does this account of the "first" Thanksgiving differ from our modern-day celebration? Are there any traditions from the first event that you'd like to celebrate today? Identify these traditions and explain your reasons.

A Member of the Wampanoag Tribe

Although there are no written accounts from any member of the Wampanoag tribe who were at the feast, I was fortunate to be able to speak with a current member of the Wampanoag tribe during a recent trip to Martha's Vineyard, Massachusetts.

Question: What do you think about what some Americans call "The First Thanksgiving?"

Answer: The problem is that Natives have always had different ceremonies for thanksgiving. It may have been this one, it may have been that one. Any truth that it would have historically would be just the act, not the specific date. We have always been thankful for everything. To tie it to a specific event is inappropriate. [The Wampanoag gave thanks for] different seasons, different crops.

Question: How do members of the Wampanoag tribe view the Thanksgiving holiday today?

Answer: Some people appreciate the noticing, the interaction, the peaceful nature. Then some people are resentful that it would be viewed as such a holiday. But we all agree that it represents just a brief point in time.

THINK ABOUT IT

What would you ask a member of the Wampanoag tribe if you had the chance? Why would you ask this?

Excerpt From *Mourt's Relation*

BY EDWARD WINSLOW

Edward Winslow traveled on the *Mayflower* in 1620. He was one of the leaders on the ship and also at Plimoth Colony. His account of "The First Thanksgiving" is one of only two that survive. This is called a "primary source" because these are the actual words of someone in history.

Our harvest being gotten in, our governour sent foure men on fowling, that so we might after a speciall manner rejoice together, after we had gathered the fruits of our labours; they foure in one day killed as much fowle, as with a little helpe beside, served the Company almost a weeke, at which time amongst other Recreations, we exercised our Armes, many of the Indians coming amongst us, and amongst the rest their greatest king Massasoyt, with some ninetie men, whom for three dayes we entertained and fested, and they went out and killed five Deere, which they brought to the Plantation and bestowed on our Governour, and upon the Captaine and others. And although it be not always so plentifull, as it was at this time with us, yet by the goodness of God, we are so farre from want, that we often wish you partakers of our plentie.

Translated to modern English:

"Once our harvest came in, our governor sent four men hunting, so we might celebrate together after working so hard. Four men killed enough fowl in one day, with very little help, to serve everyone for almost a week. Along with some other sports, we practiced shooting our guns. About ninety Indians and their greatest king, Massasoit, joined us. For three days we entertained and feasted with them. They went out and killed five deer, which they brought to the Plantation and gave to our Governor, the Captain, and others. And even though we don't always have as much food as we did during this time, by the goodness of God, we are so far from want, that we often wish you could join us here."

THINK ABOUT IT

What might be different in this telling from the Thanksgiving you imagine? What is similar? What is this author's perspective on the event?

Excerpt From *Of Plimoth Plantation*

BY WILLIAM BRADFORD

William Bradford was one of the founders of Plimoth Colony. He was also its longtime governor.

They begane now to gather in ye small harvest they had, and to fitte up their houses and dwellings against winter, being well recovered in health and strength, and had all things in good plenty; For as some were thus imployed in affairs abroad, others were exercised in fishing, aboute codd, and bass, and other fish, of which yey tooke good store, of which every family had their portion. All ye somer ther was no want. And now begane to come in store of foule, as winter approached, of which this place did abound when they came first (but afterward decreased by degrees). And besids water foule, ther was great store of wild Turkies, of which they tooke many besids venison, & Besids, they had about a peck a meale a weeke to a person, or now since harvest, Indean corn to that proportion. Which made many afterwards write so largly of their plenty hear to their friends in England, which were not fained, but true reports.

Translated to modern English:

"They began to gather in the small harvest they had, and to prepare their houses for winter. We were all well recovered in health and strength and had a good amount of food. Some of us had business overseas. Others fished and caught a lot of cod, bass, and other fish. Every family received a good portion of fish. All summer, everyone had enough to eat. We were beginning to store up fowl, as winter approached. There were many fowl when we first came here, but after a while, there weren't as many. Besides waterfowl, there was great store of wild turkeys, of which they took many, and venison, etc. They also had about 16 pints of meal a week to a person. And since the harvest, they also had that much Indian corn. Many people wrote to their friends in England, telling them about all of the food they had. The reports they wrote were true."

THINK ABOUT IT

Compare this account to Winslow's account on page 59. Are the Wampanoag mentioned? What might this say about this author's perspective on the event?

The First Thanksgiving, 1621

Unfortunately, there are no written records from the Wampanoag perspective of the "first" Thanksgiving. However, several artists have depicted their own versions of the event in paintings. Many aspects of these works include errors. For example, in the painting below, the Wampanoag are dressed as Plains Indians, with large, feathered headdresses.

by Jean Leon Jerome Ferris (early 1900s)

THINK ABOUT IT

1. What do you notice about how the Wampanoag and the English are seated in this painting? What might this say about how the English saw the Wampanoag and how the Wampanoag saw the English? Is it a way to show English superiority or simply a difference in cultures?

2. Look at the faces of the English woman guiding the Wampanoag woman on the left and the English woman standing at the table. What might the women be feeling and thinking at this point? Describe how some of the men might be feeling, based on their expressions.

3. Look at the child in this painting. How might her perspective be different from that of the child in the third painting on page 63?

The First Thanksgiving

Even though Jennie Brownscombe tried hard to be accurate in her paintings, there are still some details that are not correct. One example is that the Native Americans pictured are wearing Sioux Indian headdresses. Also, the log cabin shown was not true to the times.

by Jennie Brownscombe, 1914

THINK ABOUT IT

Compare and contrast this painting to *The First Thanksgiving, 1621* by Ferris. What is similar? What is different? What do you notice about where the focus is in the painting? What might this say about the perspective of the painter?

Untitled

While our modern Thanksgiving dinner usually includes turkey, mashed potatoes, and stuffing, the historical meal included various water birds, such as duck, as well as venison (deer meat), porridge, and corn.

title, artist, and date unknown

THINK ABOUT IT

1. Compare this painting to the first two. What is different about the seating arrangements? What does this say about the perspective of the painter?

2. Look at the child in this painting. How might her perspective be different from that of the child in the Ferris painting? Why do you think the artist chose to show her this way?

GRAPHIC ORGANIZER **Name** ______________________ **Date** ______________

DIFFERENT VIEWS OF THANKSGIVING

The texts and paintings offer different views of the "first" Thanksgiving.
What conclusions can you draw about that event?

Text/Painting	What can you conclude?	What effect does it have on you?

Conclusions: ____

____

____

REVOLUTIONARY WAR

(King George III vs. the American Colonists)

In the 1700s, the British monarchy needed money to support its army. It imposed taxes on the American colonists to raise that money. Taxes were put on paper goods, sugar, tea, and other items. The colonists did not think this was fair. They had no say in the matter but thought they should. Eventually, they decided to declare independence from King George III and Great Britain.

TEXTS

The Revolutionary War

Our lives might be very different today if it weren't for the Revolutionary War. This text explains how that war began and its effect on the development of our nation.

April 19, 1775, marked the end of an era. On that day, British troops fired on American colonists in Lexington and Concord, Massachusetts. This was the beginning of the American Revolution. The war started as a fight for the rights of English people in Britain's 13 American colonies. But those people soon declared—and won—their independence from Britain. They created a new nation—the United States of America.

Background of the Revolution

Britain established its first colony in North America in 1607. By the early 1760s, there were 13 colonies. These were Connecticut, Delaware, Georgia, Maryland, Massachusetts, New Hampshire, New Jersey, New York, North Carolina, Pennsylvania, Rhode Island, South Carolina, and Virginia. About 1.5 million colonists lived there. The colonies were far away from Britain, and they were used to running their own affairs. Each had its own assembly. They ran the everyday business of the colonies and collected taxes. Britain rarely taxed the Americans.

The French and Indian War (1754–63) changed that. Britain won that war against France. But the war was costly, and Britain owed a lot of money. Britain also needed money to keep up its army in North America. The British government therefore decided to tax the Americans.

The British Parliament passed the Stamp Act in 1765. It taxed newspapers and almost everything else that was printed. This angered the colonists. Why, they asked, should we pay taxes to Britain?

The colonists decided to fight against the taxes. Representatives of nine of the colonies met in New York in 1765. They formed the Stamp Act Congress. It said the colonists should boycott (refuse to buy) British goods. Groups called the Sons of Liberty also fought against British taxes. They often used violence against British tax collectors.

The colonists' opposition forced Parliament to repeal (withdraw) the Stamp Act. This made the colonists aware of their power. Other British attempts to impose new taxes only made things worse.

Boston was the center of opposition to Britain's tax policies. In 1770, a raggedy crowd of people taunted some British soldiers. The frightened soldiers shot into the crowd, killing five Americans. The Boston Massacre, as it was called, led to a new boycott.

Continued on next page >>

Parliament again gave in. It removed all taxes except for one on tea, the most popular drink in the colonies. The Americans were outraged. On the night of December 16, 1773, a group of men boarded British ships in Boston Harbor. They threw the cargoes of tea overboard. This action became known as the Boston Tea Party.

The British Parliament then passed four harsh measures in 1774. The colonists called them the Intolerable Acts. The acts closed the port of Boston. They took away many of Massachusetts' rights of self-government. And they allowed British troops to be housed in private homes.

These measures only served to unite the colonists. More and more of them felt that their basic liberties were at stake. In 1774, representatives of all the colonies except Georgia met in Philadelphia at the First Continental Congress. They tried to get Britain to resolve the issues peacefully. But they were ready to fight if it became necessary.

The War Begins

The American Revolution is also called the Revolutionary War and the American War of Independence. The first shots of that war were fired on April 19, 1775. British troops were in Lexington, Massachusetts, searching for hidden arms. Waiting for the British were 77 minutemen. They were colonists who were trained to be "ready in a minute." No one knows who fired first. But eight Americans were killed. That same day, British and American soldiers fought again at nearby Concord. The news spread through the colonies, which quickly prepared for war.

But not all colonists were ready for a complete break with Britain. Hundreds of thousands were still loyal to Britain and its king. They opposed independence. They were known as Loyalists or Tories. Hundreds of thousands of other colonists were neutral. They were not sure if they wanted a complete break with Britain.

The question of independence was finally decided at the Second Continental Congress. That Congress began in Philadelphia on May 1775, the month after the fighting started. At first, the delegates were just as divided as the rest of the colonists. They debated the issue for more than a year. Finally, the delegates adopted the Declaration of Independence on July 4, 1776. It declared that the 13 colonies were "free and independent states."

THINK ABOUT IT

Do you think boycotts are a good way of protesting against something? Why or why not? If you could boycott something today, what would it be and why?

Revolutionary War. (2016). *The New Book of Knowledge.* Retrieved January 26, 2016, from Grolier Online. http://nbk.grolier.com/ncpage?tn=/encyc/article.html=01000150

Excerpt From *Common Sense*

BY THOMAS PAINE

In January 1776, colonist Thomas Paine published *Common Sense*, a political pamphlet that argued for American independence. His views sum up the perspective of many colonists nicely. Here, Paine speaks out against a monarchy.

For all men being originally equals, no one by birth could have a right to set up his own family in perpetual preference to all others forever, and tho' himself might deserve some decent degree of honours of his contemporaries, yet his descendants might be far too unworthy to inherit them.

Paine then goes on to say that it may make sense for small islands like Great Britain to have a king, but not whole continents.

Small islands, not capable of protecting themselves, are the proper objects for kingdoms to take under their care; but there is something very absurd, in supposing a continent to be perpetually governed by an island.

THINK ABOUT IT

1. What are your thoughts about monarchies and rulers coming from the same family? Are your opinions different from or similar to Thomas Paine's?

2. Do you agree with Paine in that it is okay for small islands to be ruled by kings, but not big continents? Why or why not?

COMMON SENSE;

ADDRESSED TO THE

INHABITANTS

OF

AMERICA,

On the following interesting

SUBJECTS.

I. Of the Origin and Design of Government in general, with concise Remarks on the English Constitution.

II. Of Monarchy and Hereditary Succession.

III. Thoughts on the present State of American Affairs.

IV. Of the present Ability of America, with some miscellaneous Reflections.

Man knows no Master save creating HEAVEN,
Or those whom choice and common good ordain.
THOMSON.

PHILADELPHIA;

Printed, and Sold, by R. BELL, in Third-Street,

MDCCLXXVI.

A Father and Son Debate

There are always at least two sides to every story, and the story of the Revolutionary War is no exception. Sometimes, even members of the same family had different perspectives when it came to England and its colonies across the ocean. One such family was the Franklin family—Benjamin Franklin and his son William, actually. While both men wanted what was best for the colonies, they differed in how they thought that could be achieved. This play is historically based, but a modern take on a conversation this father and son might have had.

Characters:
William Franklin, Benjamin Franklin's son; Royal Governor of New Jersey

Ben Franklin, William's father; one of the founding fathers of the United States

---

Setting: Benjamin Franklin's home in Pennsylvania

William: Dad, can we talk?

Ben: Of course, son. What's on your mind?

William: Well, Mother told me you think that King George was responsible for the Tea Act and not Parliament. Is that true?

Ben: Actually, yes. I do think that it was the king who decided to tax the tea we in America receive from England.

William: I hope you're not starting to agree with those Patriots, are you? Do you really think America should separate from England?

Ben: William, like you, I want what's best for the colonies. But I'm starting to disagree with the way England is running things over here. Maybe we'd be better off as an independent nation.

William: But Dad, independence will mean one thing—anarchy. People will run wild! Without the colonies having England's support, all we'll have is chaos! The colonies depend on the king. We can still live in harmony!

Ben: I'm starting to think that's not possible, William. I'm just not sure anymore if the people of the colonies owe complete obedience to the king. I have tried to get the British government to change their ways, but they refused to listen.

William: Are you saying you're willing to go against the king?

Ben: Look, William, I like King George, always have. But things are different now. The colonies are becoming more powerful, perhaps even a rival to England.

William: Rival? It sounds like you might support a war with Britain. I, for one, would rather have stability than anarchy.

Ben: Son, we're just going to have to agree to disagree on this one and wait to see how this all turns out.

> **THINK ABOUT IT**
> What are some of the main points Ben Franklin makes in support of an independent nation? What are some of the main points William Franklin makes against it?

Name _____ Date _____

NAME CALLING

King George III along with many British thought the American colonists were traitors. What might the British say to prove this?

How might an American colonist respond to the British?

American Colonist

British

10 MUST-HAVE TEXT SETS © Carol Pugliano-Martin, Scholastic Inc.

AFRICAN AMERICANS, NATIVE AMERICANS, AND WOMEN IN THE REVOLUTIONARY WAR

There were many people who participated in the American Revolution, but some historians have tended not to include them. Some examples of these participants are African Americans, Native Americans, and women.

TEXTS

The Unsung Heroes and Heroines

We all know the stories of General George Washington and the other founding fathers. But there were many other groups of people who contributed to the Revolutionary War. We should know their stories, too.

George Washington and Thomas Jefferson were members of the upper class that participated in the Revolutionary War. Most of the stories we read about the war center around men like them. But not only the upper class was involved; the middle and lower classes were also on the battlefield, putting their lives in great danger for what they believed in.

The classes were not treated the same. When the middle and lower classes were taken prisoner, they were sent to prison ships. The rich who were captured were put on parole and allowed to live their everyday lives. The middle- and lower-class soldiers suffered most from hunger, illness, and poverty. At the end of the war, if they had survived, they struggled to carry on with their lives. Many of these men were not given the land or money they were promised for fighting in the war.

Free African Americans, enslaved Africans, and Native Americans played an important role in the American Revolution, too. Many African Americans fought on either the Loyalists' (King George III's) side or the Patriots' (colonists') side. Native Americans also had to choose which side to support.

Some enslaved African Americans and Native Americans fought on the Loyalists' side because the Loyalists gave them a feeling of protection.

The Loyalists also promised the slaves their freedom if they joined their side. The Loyalists also promised Native Americans that their land would not be taken away from them. At the end of the war, neither of these groups got all the rewards they were promised. Many enslaved Africans remained enslaved. Native Americans lost their independence and their land.

Women played an important role in the Revolution as well. Some women went to the military camps to help feed and care for the soldiers. Other women took charge of businesses while their husbands were away fighting. Although women were not allowed to fight, some helped to load cannons. One woman did fight, though. Deborah Sampson joined the military under the name of Robert Shurtleff. She was a very strong woman, so she was able to perform most of the same duties as a man. Although women participated in the war, they did not receive the freedom or equality promised by the Declaration of Independence or the Constitution. Women would not be allowed to vote until 1920.

THINK ABOUT IT

Why don't we hear much about these groups? Are things different today? Explain why or why not.

Revolutionary War. (2016). *The New Book of Knowledge*. Retrieved January 26, 2016, from Grolier Online. http://nbk.grolier.com/ncpage?tn=/encyc/article.html=01000150

The following texts show the perspective of African-American participation in the Revolutionary War. We hear from the Loyalist side, the Patriot side, a former soldier, and a modern-day government leader.

Proclamation From Lord Dunmore, a Loyalist

During the Revolutionary War, enslaved African Americans were torn between sides. Each side, Loyalists and Patriots, promised freedom to slaves who would support their side. The Governor of Virginia, a Loyalist whose title was Lord Dunmore, realized that if he recruited slaves to fight for his cause, it would weaken the Patriots. Here, he promises freedom to those who would be willing to fight for King George III.

*A*nd I hereby further declare all indented servants, Negroes, or others (appertaining to Rebels) free, that are able and willing to bear arms, they joining His Majesty's Troops, as soon as may be, for the more speedily reducing the Colony to a proper sense of their duty, to this Majesty's crown and dignity.

– Lord Dunmore, November 1775

THINK ABOUT IT

What do you think of this offer from Lord Dunmore? If you were enslaved, would you have taken him up on his offer even though it meant fighting against independence from Britain? Tell why. Can you understand why many enslaved African Americans fought for the British? Explain.

Declaration From a Meeting of the Virginia Assembly

Within one month of Lord Dunmore's 1775 proclamation, about 300 slaves joined the Loyalist forces. This angered the slaveholders of Virginia. The Virginia Assembly retaliated by threatening to execute slaves who took Lord Dunmore up on his offer.

. . . all negro or other slaves, conspiring to rebel or make insurrection, shall suffer death. . . . We think it proper to declare that all slaves who have been, or shall be seduced, by his lordship's proclamation . . . to desert their masters' service, and take up arms against the inhabitants of this colony, shall be liable to such punishment as shall hereafter be directed by the General Convention. We hereby promise pardon to them, they surrendering themselves to . . . any . . . commander of our troops, and not appearing in arms after the publication thereof.

– Representatives of the People of the Colony and Dominion of Virginia, assembled in General Convention. Virginia, December 14, 1775

THINK ABOUT IT

What do you think this phrase means: ". . . all slaves who have been seduced by his lordship's proclamation"? (See Lord Dunmore's Proclamation on page 75.)

Letter From Lt. Col. Henry Laurens

At first, George Washington was against recruiting enslaved African Americans for fighting. However, when the Patriots saw the benefits of arming the African Americans, Lieutenant Colonel Henry Laurens made this appeal in a letter to George Washington on March 16, 1779.

*O*ur affairs in the Southern department [are] in more favorable light than we had viewed them in a few days ago. Nevertheless, the Country is greatly distressed, and will be more so, unless further reinforcements are sent to its relief. Had we Arms for 3000 such black Men, as I could select in Carolina, I should have no doubt of success in driving the British out of Georgia and subduing East Florida before the end of July.

Some leaders were afraid that the enslaved African Americans would turn on them. However, Washington saw that Dunmore's proclamation was bringing enslaved African Americans into the British army and increasing its numbers. Washington decided to do the same. Eventually about 5,000 free and enslaved African Americans served in the American army.

Many slaves who fought for both sides did receive their freedom in return. But many others did not.

THINK ABOUT IT

Where does Lt. Col. Laurens mention the reason for the need to recruit enslaved African Americans to fight? Do you think it is fair that the Loyalists and Patriots recruited these African Americans to fight in the war? Try to defend all sides: enslaved Africans who fought for the Patriots or the Loyalists, those who refused to fight for either side, and Patriots and Loyalists.

Letter From Peter Kiteridge, 1806

Peter Kiteridge, a former slave who fought in the Revolution for the American side, asks for some payment to help support his wife and four children. He feels he is deserving of it after his service. I was unable to find out if he ever did get paid.

In the year of our Lord 1775 or 6 and in the twenty fifth of my age I entered into the service of the U.S. as a private soldier wherein I continued five years and contracted a complaint from which I have suffered in a greater or less degree ever since and with which I am now afflicted . . . At present having arrived at the fifty eight year of my life and afflicted with severe and as I apprehend with incurable diseases where by the labor of my hands is wholy cut off, and with it is the only means of my support. My family at this time consists of a wife and four children, three of whom are so young as to be unable to support themselves and the time of their mother is wholly occupied in taking care of myself & my little ones—Thus gentlemen, in this my extremity I am induced to call on you for assistance. . . .

THINK ABOUT IT

What physical problems does Peter Kiteridge say he suffers from? Look at the year of Kiteridge's letter. What does this tell you about how he was treated after the war?

General Colin Powell

General Colin Powell, United States Secretary of State from 2001–2005, presents his views on the recruitment of slaves for service in the Revolutionary War.

*W*hen war comes and blood is being shed and casualties are being experienced, you really have to start looking for manpower. And by now, it is known that slaves can be soldiers. . . . And the British were trying to recruit blacks, promising them their freedom. So as was often the case in our history, market forces—isn't that a horrible way to put it?—market forces became operative for purposes of strategic necessity. And so black men were recruited, and it was determined that they could be good soldiers. So necessity has always pushed us along.

THINK ABOUT IT

"Market forces" are the effects of supply and demand on trading. They refer to goods and resources. What were the market forces Powell is talking about? Powell says using this term is horrible. Why do you think he feels this way?

Native Americans in the Revolutionary War

Like African Americans, Native Americans were torn between the two sides in the Revolutionary War. However, they tended to side more strongly with the British because the British promised Native Americans they would not lose their land.

Speech by the Second Continental Congress

In the beginning of the war, the Patriots urged Native Americans to stay neutral in the struggle. This speech was directed to the Six Nations—the Mohawks, Oneidas, Tuscaroras, Onondagas, Cayugas, and Senecas.

We desire you will hear and receive what we have now told you, and that you will open a good ear and listen to what we are now going to say. This is a family quarrel between us and Old England. You Indians are not concerned in it. We don't wish you to take up the hatchet against the king's troops. We desire you to remain at home, and not join on either side, but keep the hatchet buried deep.

– The Second Continental Congress,
Speech to the Six Nations, July 13, 1775

THINK ABOUT IT

What is the tone of this speech? Does it sound like the Continental Congress is being respectful to the Native Americans or not? Tell why. If you were a Native American at the time, how would you feel?

PRIMARY SOURCE

Burgoyne Poem

The British were very enthusiastic about recruiting Native Americans to fight for their side, as this poem by General John Burgoyne, Deputy of the British forces in Canada, reveals.

I will let loose the dogs of hell,
Ten thousand Indians, who shall yell
And foam and tear, and grin and roar,
And drench their moccasins in gore:
To these I'll give full scope and play
From Ticonderog to Florida . . .

THINK ABOUT IT

What is the tone of this poem? If you were a Native American reading this, what would you think about it? Give evidence from the poem in your answer.

Speech by Thayendanegea (Joseph Brant)

Thayendanegea, also known as Joseph Brant, was a Mohawk military and political leader who lived in what is now New York state. Here is an excerpt of a speech he delivered in London before Lord George Germaine, British secretary of state, on March 14, 1776. Brant spoke of broken promises by the British.

Brother, the Mohawks have on all occasions shown their zeal and loyalty to the great king. Yet they have been very badly treated by the people in that country. The city of Albany has laid an unjust claim to the lands on which our lower castle is built. We were told that the king and wise men here would do us justice. But this has never been done and it makes us feel uneasy. We request that his majesty will attend to this matter. It troubles our nation and we cannot sleep easy in our beds. Indeed, it is very hard, when we have let the king's subjects have so much land for so little value, they should want to cheat us in this manner of the small spots we have left for our women and children to live on. We are tired of making complaints and getting no redress. We therefore hope that we will get justice.

THINK ABOUT IT

What is it like to hear the firsthand perspective of a Native American? How does it affect your thoughts on the subject of Native Americans in the Revolutionary War? Use evidence from Brant's speech to support your answer.

Congressional Committee Report

Eventually, Native Americans realized that an independent America was more of a threat to them than continued British rule. The British were trying to prevent colonists from settling in the West. If America became independent, there was no telling what would become of Native American lands. After the war was over, the United States Congress made it very clear how it felt about the Native Americans supporting the British.

The Indian tribes by joining the British in the Revolution had forfeited their rights to possession of lands within the United States; the new country would be justified in compelling the Indians to retire to Canada or to the unknown areas beyond the Mississippi river.

– U.S. Congress, 1783–1784

THINK ABOUT IT

Take the perspective of a Native American during the Revolutionary War. Whose side would you be on? Or would you remain neutral? Explain why.

Women in the Revolutionary War

Just as African Americans and Native Americans were discriminated against, women were not viewed as equals either. They assisted during the war, but they weren't able to take advantage of the freedom that was earned after the war was over. It would be about 150 years before women would receive the right to vote.

Letter From Abigail Adams

Before becoming president, John Adams was a member of the Continental Congress. His wife, Abigail Adams, was an activist in her own right. In this letter written in 1776, she pleads with her husband to make sure that the new independent nation, if they are successful in achieving one, gives women more rights.

ABIGAIL ADAMS.

I long to hear that you have declared an independency— and, by the way, in the new Code of Laws which I suppose it will be necessary for you to make, I desire you would Remember the Ladies and be more generous and favorable to them than your ancestors. Do not put such unlimited power into the hands of the Husbands. Remember, all Men would be tyrants if they could. If particular care and attention is not paid to the Ladies, we are determined to foment a Rebellion, and will not hold ourselves bound by any Laws in which we have no voice or Representation.

–Abigail Adams, March 31, 1776

THINK ABOUT IT
Put Abigail Adams' letter into your own words. What is she asking her husband to do?

Interview With Deborah Sampson

Some women took their desire for involvement one step further. Deborah Sampson dressed as a man and became a Patriot soldier during the Revolutionary War. She was later discovered and removed from service. Here is a fictional, but fact-based, interview with Deborah Sampson about her participation in the Revolutionary War.

Reporter: Ms. Sampson, thank you so much for speaking with me today.

Sampson: You're quite welcome. I'm very happy to be able to tell my story.

Reporter: Why did you choose to dress as a man to fight for independence?

Sampson: It was not enough for me to help behind the scenes as many women did. I am not criticizing them. What they did was very important. But it wasn't enough for me. I so believed in the quest for independence from England, I had to fight myself.

Reporter: Weren't you terrified of war?

Sampson: I was more terrified of living under British rule forever.

Reporter: You were wounded during the war. Do you regret what you did at all?

Sampson: Not at all. I am glad that I swerved from the path of female delicacy to become a hero. It wasn't enough to live in a state of punishment. I would do it again!

DEBORAH SIMPSON PRESENTING THE LETTER TO GENERAL WASHINGTON.

THINK ABOUT IT

1. If you were a woman during the Revolutionary War, would you have gotten involved? Explain your reasons.

2. How do you think Deborah Sampson felt about being a woman during the time she was living in? What clues does she give in the interview? How might it have felt to not have the same rights as men?

WHO WANTED WHAT IN THE REVOLUTIONARY WAR?

Each of these key groups in the Revolutionary War wanted something. Knowing what each group wanted helps to understand the war better. Use information from the texts to fill in the chart.

What African Americans Wanted	What England Wanted	What Colonial or Federal Government Wanted

What Native Americans Wanted	What England Wanted	What Colonial or Federal Government Wanted

What Women Wanted

TEXT SET
10
Historical Events

RATIFICATION OF THE UNITED STATES CONSTITUTION

The United States Constitution tells how the federal government works. Each state also has its own constitution. The constitution of each state is the highest law for that state—but the U.S. Constitution is the highest law of the land.

The U.S. Constitution was adopted and signed in September 1787. Then it had to be ratified by nine of the thirteen states before it became official. On June 21, 1788, New Hampshire became the ninth state to ratify the Constitution. It was agreed that government under the U.S. Constitution would begin on March 4, 1789. By 1790, all the thirteen states had ratified the Constitution.

TEXTS

Why the Constitution Matters

President Barack Obama spoke with *Scholastic News* about how a document written in 1787 still guides our nation today. He sat down in 2011 with *Scholastic News* Kid Reporters Jacob Schroeder, 12, and Topanga Sena, 10, at the White House to talk about why the Constitution is still so important—to adults and kids.

Jacob: Why is the Constitution important to kids today?

President Obama: It is an amazing document. When you think about our country, unlike most countries, we're not all of the same race or religion. We don't all come from the same places. Many of us are immigrants. But what holds us all together is a belief in certain ideals and certain values.

The Constitution really is what sets us apart by saying that every single person is treated with respect; every single individual has certain rights; and that the government has to follow certain rules in how it interacts with its citizens. So it sets out a model not only for our democracy, but also for how each of us has certain individual freedoms and certain rights that can't be broken.

The best example is freedom of speech, which, since you guys are reporters, you have to be concerned about. It's because of our Constitution that newspapers and radio and television reporters are able to find out what's happening. They can ask questions of elected officials. They can write criticisms about what officials are doing. In a lot of countries, that's not true. But our Constitution says that's a right that's important to us.

Topanga: The Constitution is more than 220 years old. Why is it still cool now?

President Obama: Well, I think it's very cool to have a document that—even though it was written [more than] 220 years ago—still applies today.

The Founders were trying to solve problems that all human societies have to deal with. We all need a government to make sure that we can live together in an orderly fashion. But we don't want the people in power to be able to tell us what to do across the board. Instead, we have a system where we, the people, are able to tell the government what we think is best.

If it weren't for the Constitution, a lot of the things that we take for granted—[such as] our ability to speak our minds, our ability to worship any religion that we want—wouldn't be around. So I think that's pretty cool, because there are a lot of societies that don't have those protections.

THINK ABOUT IT

For more than 220 years, America has been governed by the same document. What does that say about America, its people, and this document?

Alexander Hamilton vs. Patrick Henry

Did you know that the leaders of the young United States did not feel very united when it came to agreeing on our Constitution? If two of them were alive today, how would they explain themselves? Let's hear an imaginary, fact-based argument between Alexander Hamilton, who was a Federalist, or a supporter of a strong central government, and Patrick Henry, an Anti-Federalist, who was against a central government.

Hamilton: We need a strong central government. We cannot have each of the 13 states running itself. The states should work toward a common goal—to make our new country strong. We don't want individual groups fighting for their own best interests against the will of all of the people.

Henry: We fought the American Revolution to get away from a domineering central government. What you are suggesting sounds a lot like England's monarchy.

Hamilton: No, it is absolutely not! We cannot function properly if every state chooses when to go or not go to war or to borrow money for military needs. Unlike in a monarchy, the people will have a voice, but the final decisions must be made by a central government or else there will be total chaos!

Henry: I smell a rat! Where are the rights of individuals? If that one central government is making the final decisions, who is to say that the people in each state will get equal treatment? It should be every state for itself if we don't want to be ruled by a king or queen! Our rights and privileges will be endangered! It will be tyranny!

Hamilton: It is not tyranny that we want—only a just, fair, limited federal government.

Alexander Hamilton

Patrick Henry

Continued on next page >>

Henry: What do you mean by "limited?" It sounds like you're saying the federal government would have all the power.

Hamilton: No, you misunderstand. Each state will have its own senators and governors. Those leaders will look out for the needs of each individual state. But when it comes to major decisions that will affect the whole union, there must be one deciding branch. If we let each state's passions rule, we will not be able to make rational decisions for the better of the country.

Henry: But you make it sound like people are foolish and are only led by emotion. You really underestimate the intelligence of the average person to make a rational decision. The Constitution was not written so that the government could control the people. It was written so that the people could control the government. If people don't have control, the government will rule every aspect of our lives!

Hamilton: We will create three branches of our national government. Each branch will have a different job. Each branch will check the other two. This way, no one group will overpower the others.

Henry: It's beginning to sound a bit better. But it's not enough. I don't think every state should agree to this Constitution unless you add more about individual rights.

Hamilton: I don't believe that we need to do that.

Henry: We must find a way around this. Perhaps a compromise?*

That compromise was the Bill of Rights, which protects the rights of individual citizens. It was added to the Constitution in 1791.

THINK ABOUT IT

1. Put yourself in Patrick Henry's shoes. Try to explain to a partner how a constitution without a section for individual rights would be like a monarchy.

2. Think of a time when you had to convince someone that your idea was the best one. How was your situation similar to or different from Alexander Hamilton's argument with Patrick Henry?

3. Now try to remember a time when you had to make a compromise with someone. How did it work out? Explain whether the compromise made the situation better.

    10 MUST-HAVE TEXT SETS © Carol Pugliano-Martin, Scholastic Inc.

The Three Branches of the United States Government

The creators of the United States Constitution wanted to divide power within the federal government. They did not want these powers to be controlled by just one person or one group. The creators were afraid that if a small group received too much power, the United States would fall under the rule of another dictator or tyrant. To avoid that risk, the new government was divided into three parts, or branches: the executive branch, the legislative branch, and the judicial branch.

How Our Government Works
The Three Branches of Government

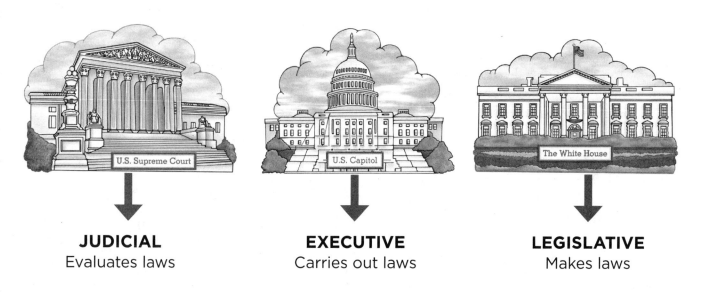

JUDICIAL
Evaluates laws

EXECUTIVE
Carries out laws

LEGISLATIVE
Makes laws

THINK ABOUT IT
Explain how having three branches of government prevents our country from becoming a dictatorship.

The Bill of Rights

In 1789, the First Congress of the United States proposed 12 amendments to the Constitution. Of these, ten (Articles 3 to 12) were ratified, or approved, by the majority of state legislatures on December 15, 1791. These first 10 amendments to the Constitution are called the Bill of Rights. It outlines the basic rights and freedoms of American citizens, including freedom of religion, speech, and the press.

Congress of the United States, begun and held at the City of New-York, on Wednesday the fourth of March, one thousand seven hundred and eighty nine.

THE Conventions of a number of the States, having at the time of their adopting the Constitution, expressed a desire, in order to prevent misconstruction or abuse of its powers, that further declaratory and restrictive clauses should be added: And as extending the ground of public confidence in the Government, will best ensure the beneficent ends of its institution.

RESOLVED by the Senate and House of Representatives of the United States of America, in Congress assembled, two thirds of both Houses concurring, that the following Articles be proposed to the Legislatures of the several States, as amendments to the Constitution of the United States, all, or any of which Articles, when ratified by three fourths of the said Legislatures, to be valid to all intents and purposes, as part of the said Constitution; viz.

ARTICLES in addition to, and Amendment of the Constitution of the United States of America, proposed by Congress, and ratified by the Legislatures of the several States, pursuant to the fifth Article of the original Constitution.

Continued on next page >>

Article the third...   Congress shall make no law respecting an establishment of religion, or prohibiting the free exercise thereof; or abridging the freedom of speech, or of the press; or the right of the people peaceably to assemble, and to petition the Government for a redress of grievances.

Article the fourth...   A well regulated Militia, being necessary to the security of a free State, the right of the people to keep and bear Arms, shall not be infringed.

Article the fifth...   No Soldier shall, in time of peace be quartered in any house, without the consent of the Owner, nor in time of war, but in a manner to be prescribed by law.

Article the sixth...   The right of the people to be secure in their persons, houses, papers, and effects, against unreasonable searches and seizures, shall not be violated, and no Warrants shall issue, but upon probable cause, supported by Oath or affirmation, and particularly describing the place to be searched, and the persons or things to be seized.

Article the seventh...   No person shall be held to answer for a capital, or otherwise infamous crime, unless on a presentment or indictment of a Grand Jury, except in cases arising in the land or naval forces, or in the Militia, when in actual service in time of War or public danger; nor shall any person be subject for the same offence to be twice put in jeopardy of life or limb; nor shall be compelled in any criminal case to be a witness against himself, nor be deprived of life, liberty, or property, without due process of law; nor shall private property be taken for public use, without just compensation.

Article the eighth...   In all criminal prosecutions, the accused shall enjoy the right to a speedy and public trial, by an impartial jury of the State and district wherein the crime shall have been committed, which district shall have been previously ascertained by law, and to be informed of the nature and cause of the accusation; to be confronted with the witnesses against him; to have compulsory process for obtaining witnesses in his favor, and to have the Assistance of Counsel for his defence.

Continued on next page >>

Article the ninth…   In suits at common law, where the value in controversy shall exceed twenty dollars, the right of trial by jury shall be preserved, and no fact tried by a jury, shall be otherwise re-examined in any Court of the United States, than according to the rules of the common law.

Article the tenth…   Excessive bail shall not be required, nor excessive fines imposed, nor cruel and unusual punishments inflicted.

Article the eleventh…   The enumeration in the Constitution, of certain rights, shall not be construed to deny or disparage others retained by the people.

Article the twelfth…   The powers not delegated to the United States by the Constitution, nor prohibited by it to the States, are reserved to the States respectively, or to the people.

ATTEST,
Frederick Augustus Muhlenberg, Speaker of the House of Representatives
John Adams, Vice-President of the United States, and President of the Senate
John Beckley, Clerk of the House of Representatives.
Sam. A Otis, Secretary of the Senate

THINK ABOUT IT
Which amendment to the Constitution do you think is the most important? It's a tough choice! What are the reasons for your choice?

SUM IT UP

Hamilton and Henry brought up a lot of points in their debate about the Constitution.
Fill in the speech balloons with highlights of their debate.

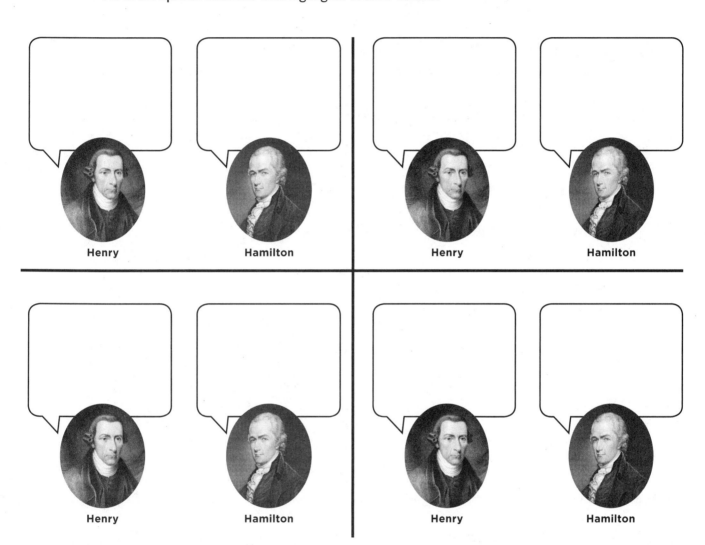

Henry   Hamilton   Henry   Hamilton

Henry   Hamilton   Henry   Hamilton

What do you think about the Constitution? Is a central government good for our country? Explain.

_____

_____

_____

_____

Resources

These are resources I used for both my instructional unit and in writing this book. There are many more out there, but this list will give you a head start.

Picture Books

Thanksgiving:

1621: A New Look at Thanksgiving by Catherine O'Neill Grace (National Geographic Children's Books, 2004).

American Revolution:

George vs. George: The American Revolution as Seen from Both Sides by Rosalyn Schanzer (National Geographic Society, 2004).

The Split History of the American Revolution: A Perspectives Flip Book by Michael Burgan (Compass Points Books, 2012).

America's Black Founders: Revolutionary Heroes & Early Leaders with 21 Activities by Nancy I. Sanders (Chicago Review Press, 2010).

John, Paul, George & Ben by Lane Smith (Scholastic, 2009).

United States Constitution:

We the People: The Story of Our Constitution by Lynne Cheney (Simon & Schuster Books for Young Readers, 2008).

Magazines

Ask

Cobblestones

DynaMath

Faces

Geography Spin

National Geographic for Kids

Parent & Child

Scholastic News

Science Spin

SuperScience

Time for Kids

Scholastic Teacher

Professional Books

Texts and Lessons for Content Area Reading: With More Than 75 Articles from The New York Times, Rolling Stone, The Washington Post, Car and Driver, Chicago Tribune, *and Many Others* by Harvey "Smokey" Daniels and Nancy Steineke (Heinemann, 2011).

The Common Core Guidebook, Grades 3–5: Informational Text Lessons, Guided Practice, Suggested Book Lists, and Reproducible Organizers by Rozlyn Linder Ph.D. (The Literacy Initiative, 2013).

The Common Core Guidebook, Grades 6–8: Informational Text Lessons, Guided Practice, Suggested Book Lists, and Reproducible Organizers by Rozlyn Linder Ph.D. (The Literacy Initiative, 2013).

Text Sets

Council of Chief State School Officers (CCSSO) web site:

http://www.ccsso.org/Navigating_Text_Complexity/Get_the_Skinny.html (Text Set Examples)

http://www.ccsso.org/Navigating_Text_Complexity/Chart_Your_Course.html (Guide to Creating Text Sets)

Teachers College/Columbia University Reading and Writing Project web site:

http://readingandwritingproject.org/resources/text-sets